God's Guarantees for Giving

A Biblical Look at the Law of Tithing…
Was It Rescinded by Grace?

God bless

Ron Knott

Ron Knott

xulon
PRESS

Acknowledgments

First, I want to thank my Lord and Savior Jesus Christ for more than I could ever record in this book. His shed blood is worth more than all the riches of the world. The Lord spared my life so many times, especially when I was a Navy fighter pilot. This very dangerous profession claimed the lives of many of my friends who flew supersonic Navy Fighters aboard aircraft carriers. I am the only living member of my flight school graduating class. More than 200 of my buddies lost their lives flying the same type mission that I flew day after day. I have no choice but to obey my Savior on this project.

My parents taught me the gift of giving at a very early age. They owned a small country store, in a small sawmill town, that served an area of very poor people. In fact we were all poor. But, we seemed to have just a little more than most.

I observed my mother giving food to needy families who could not afford to pay. Sometimes she would allow credit to deprived families knowing that she would never be repaid. Her response was always the same, "I give them something to eat as unto the Lord." This was years before I read in the Bible (Matthew 25) that feeding the poor was the same as feeding Jesus.

My dad got up after midnight many times to take sick folks to the doctor. Many people in the area had no car or telephone. He would drive many miles to the nearest doctor, wait for them to be treated, and if necessary would pay their doctor bills. Thanks mom and dad for teaching me the spirit of giving.

I am also extremely grateful to the following family and friends who helped in writing this book.

My wife Sharon and my daughter Kristi had to give up the computer for hours for me to complete this book. They also had to endure my times of frustration when things did not go well.

A great big thank you to Michelle who spent hours researching and editing this work. I do believe she could find a printing error on a dollar bill. Her many suggestions and professional advise is appreciated. Thanks Michelle.

Ann, SoShawna, and Phil encouraged and supported this effort from the beginning. Your encouragement and assistance is appreciated.

Thanks Albert and Pat for your support. Your persuasion and urging kept me on the target of truth.

I must express my sincere appreciation to Pat Blais for her professional assistance with the entire task. Thanks Pat for my many phone calls, e-mails, and visits to get it right.

Thanks to all those who posted information on the Internet about tithing. Many did not leave their name or e-mail address. I was able to collect helpful information from these sources.

Table of Contents

Introduction

**Jesus commanded us to, *Search the Scriptures*
(John 5:39) for truth.**

I am aware that the title of this book addresses a sensitive issue for most, if not all, church organizations. The subject of money immediately gets everyone's attention; and when religious beliefs are added to the discussion, a dangerous subject matter is the result. Since money is the means by which all churches exist (one might suggest it has become their life-blood) I'm sure this book will prove quite controversial. Yet I am bold (or perhaps crazy) enough to address this very sensitive topic, which few would dare to broach. I am not fearful of controversy, for it is evidence of questions and confusion. Since God is not the author of confusion, everyone who reads this book must come to a biblically based conclusion upon which they will stand one day before His throne. Either you will agree with the message in this book, or you will disagree. You cannot remain neutral.

Review the twenty-seven reasons or considerations why Christians should not tithe; these reasons are listed below.

TWENTY SEVEN REASONS OR CONSIDERATIONS FOR NOT TITHING

1. There was no command to tithe before, or after the Law.
2. Did Adam and Eve, Job, Noah or Joseph tithe?
3. Why did God reject Cain's gift?
4. Tithing is not commanded in the Ten Commandments.
5. The tithe was never money; it was always agricultural products.
6. Tithes are to be eaten.
7. Tithes are to go into the storehouse.
8. Under the Law one could redeem his tithes.
9. Only a tenth of the tithe went to the priest.
10. Every three years the tithe went to the needy.
11. Every seven years there was no tithe.
12. The people paid a tithe to themselves.
13. Tithes were for the Levites, widows, aliens and fatherless.
14. All priests were Levites, but not all Levites were priests.
15. The Law tolerated many wives, concubines, sacrifices, and tithes. (The implication here is if we teach one of these practices—why not all?)
16. Who is robbing God of tithes and offerings?
17. Jesus did not tithe, nor did He accept tithes.
18. The New Testament Church did not tithe.
19. The New Testament command concerning giving: *Every man as he purposeth.*
20. Since the New Testament salvation plan is superior to the Old Testament salvation plan, we can conclude that the New Testament giving plan is superior to the Old Testament

giving plan. We have a better covenant with better promises. Which plan should we follow?

21. God honors acceptable gifts and rejects unacceptable gifts.
22. The Pope reinstated tithing at the Council of Macon in 585 A.D.
23. Where do your tithes go?
24. Should we support the church and the ministry? Absolutely! But not by the Old Testament Law of tithing.
25. Present day priests, pastors, and preachers are not restricted from owning land, as were their counterparts in the Old Testament.
26. Why are not all who tithe wealthy?
27. Are you blessed financially for tithing, or for giving to the poor?

Challenges of tradition are not always bad. As we see with Martin Luther, confrontation can be very positive. Millions have received the truth about the grace of God because of the stand he took. Nuggets of Bible truth have been revealed to millions that beforehand were considered heresy. Yet, these truths were in the Bible all the while, and they have withstood the test of time. They had either been overlooked or disregarded. So it is with giving for New Testament Christians. It appears that many Christian organizations have moved back under the Law.

If a person is teachable and eager to embrace God's simple TRUTH, this book will be an exciting, fresh look into Christian stewardship. You will read in this book how the Lord wants to bless you financially. And He <u>will</u> bless you, if you only obey His commands. No, this book is not about prosperity preaching by men who make big promises that seldom materialize. It is about God's guarantees for giving.

God wants us to test Him, trust Him, and prove Him and see if He will not give you more than you can contain. I am living proof of His guarantees.

Many Christians are fed spiritual junk food and as a result they have become spiritually unhealthy. In one sense, these precious children of God are weakened believers. The "bless me" club mentality has caused many sincere Christians to doubt God. Many wonder why God does not bless them when they are faithful tithe payers. Did God deceive these dedicated souls, or did man change the plan that the Lord had for Christians? Sometimes TRUTH is a wake-up call. God gave me the wake-up call about giving His way several years ago; and it has changed my life, as well as many others who have put His plan for giving into action. Read in this book how you can be blessed financially and thereby bless others by giving God's way.

I have questioned God about the poor economic conditions and the hardships that I have seen many Christians going through. These are Christians who are paying tithes without fail, but unknowingly they are not obeying the New Testament plan for giving. It is obvious that the reason they are not obeying the Lord's commands is because they do not know them. The reason they do not know them is because they are not taught correctly. In *God's Guarantees for Giving* you will be taught what the Bible says about Christian giving and God's guarantees for giving. I challenge the man-made law of New Testament tithing in this book. I have read many published works while researching this topic, however none provided specific examples of God's plan for blessings in action. Therefore I have included numerous examples throughout the book as testimony that His plan works! It is not my desire to see the flow of money into our churches decrease, in fact, as you will read in this book, I am encouraging people to give more! I hold no personal vendettas and do not want to point a finger in judgment toward any individuals or organizations. My reason for writing this book is simple. It is to provide information that I discovered while researching the subject of tithing. I have found that the message of tithing has been misinterpreted and abused by many church leaders. God calls us to be good stewards of our time and our finances, and my desire is that this book will provide a wake-up call to all who claim to follow Christ. Please read this book prayerfully with an open mind. Ask God to lead you into all TRUTH.

To test the effectiveness of the message in *God's Guarantees for Giving,* I provided a copy to ten very conservative individuals who I knew believed that New Testament tithing was as scriptural as the resurrection. They first believed that I was completely mistaken about what I had written. However, the more they read the book, and the more they studied the Scriptures, the more their understanding changed. One friend said, "Ron, this study has completely changed my mind on the subject of giving. I can't believe that I had been taught in error all these many years." All ten individuals who received the advanced copies of this manuscript urged me to publish it as a book so that TRUTH can be made known to sincere Christians.

In *God's Guarantees for Giving* I have reviewed His Book for the written procedures and commands for New Testament charitable giving. Jesus preached the following message to the Pharisees, *"You have let go of the commands of God and are holding on to the traditions of men"* (Mark 7:8-9, *NIV*). His tragic warning is still binding for us today. It is a shame to see sincere Christian leaders, faithful Christians, and dedicated churches struggling financially when the Lord wants them to prosper as He said in His Word. The pastor, the church member, and the churches are guaranteed financial blessings if they would only follow the simple commands in the Bible.

Giving is the theme of the Bible *For God so loved the world, that he **gave** His only begotten Son ...* (John 3:16). He expects us to give, as He recorded in the parable found in Luke 10:33. However, neither the preacher (priest), nor the Levite would give aid to a man in need. In fact it is recorded that the priest went to the other side of the road just to get away from the poor fellow. But, the Good Samaritan not only stopped and rendered aid to the unfortunate fellow, he placed him on his donkey, and brought him to an Inn and took care of him. He also paid the injured man's hotel bill. In other words the Samaritan was good for nothing, in that he expected "nothing" for his gift to the needy. But he impressed Jesus with this act of generosity.

You may get the impression that I am against preachers, pastors or anyone on the church payroll. That is absolutely not the case. I have a deep reverence and respect for the "Men of God." Many of them have had very little income in the early years of their pastoral career. Some of these are now reaping the financial blessing because of their many years of devoted and dedicated labor to God's work. I am delighted and excited for them to reach a position of affluence. According to the Scripture, a congregation should consider it a priority to care for the monetary needs of the church staff. If a church prospers under a pastor's ministry, that congregation should insure that the pastor's salary is sufficient. My charge to them is to teach and preach the New Testament plan of giving so all hands would be blessed. The New Testament plan does not include tithes! Please read this book prayerfully with an open mind. Ask God to lead you into all TRUTH.

Fasten your seat belts, and let's take a journey through the Bible on the subject of tithes and giving.

Part I

CHAPTER ONE

The Old Man on the Bicycle

The old man rode his wobbly bicycle to our church one cold Sunday morning. The wrinkles in his face looked like a crumpled road map. With his ruddy, leather-like skin, ruffled with deep wrinkles throughout, and his matted gray hair and beard, it was obvious that he had seen too many days in the hot sun. No teeth, either real or false, had rested on his gums for years. His clothes were tattered, dirty, and ill fitting. Most would quickly identify him as a street person who had destroyed his well being by a sinful lifestyle. That is, until you looked into his eyes. They presented a warm and loving man who just needed a little special attention. Bill's eyes related a story contrary to what his appearance portrayed.

When I saw him from a distance my first thought was, *Here is another bum wanting a handout.* However, when the worship service got underway, Bill's countenance quickly changed from that of a tired old man to one with an angelic appearance. A heavenly glow enveloped his face. His warm smile and sincere worship revealed a deep, authentic, and fervent love for God. The intrinsic nature of his worship mesmerized me.

When church ended I introduced myself to the old man and soon learned that he did not expect a handout from the church folks. He only wanted to be blessed by his Savior, and from what I observed he was truly blessed.

I asked, "Sir, is there anything that you need?" He simply replied, "My name is Bill." He gave me no last name, just Bill. Then he proceeded to tell me that he had seen angels all around the people in the church during the service. He said, "See that little girl over there? Every time she raised her hands to praise the Lord, angels rushed to her side and helped hold her arms up." That really got my attention, because the young lady he pointed out was the most dedicated and devoted young person in the church. Then he pointed out several other individuals around whom he had seen angels during the service. Bill's spiritual depth intrigued me. Someone or something was giving him authentic information to which others were apparently not attuned. I was eager to learn more from him and about him.

I asked him where he lived. He told me he lived in the middle of a cow pasture a few miles away from the city. I drove over there after church and was shocked when I saw the awful conditions of that place. His home was a camper shell for a pickup truck, which had been propped up on some old timbers so he could crawl under for shelter. That camper shell, his bicycle, and the clothes on his back were all he possessed. Wild animals had better accommodations than Bill.

Getting information out of Bill was impossible. He only wanted to talk about angels. Even so, I knew Bill was as sane as you or I. He was not mentally ill, imbalanced, or irrational. Angels seemed to be around him most of the time. Although I never saw one, I sensed the wonderful presence of peace every time I was with him.

Finally, I said, "Bill, will you let me rent you a nice, clean, warm place to stay?" I felt that is what Jesus would have done. It was not easy to persuade him, but he finally agreed. There was a mobile home park nearby that had a few homes available for rent. I rented a nice one for Bill and moved him in with his few belongings that very day. The following day I went by to see how he liked his new accommodations. I will never forget his response. He said, "I stayed in that tub for hours. The warm water felt so wonderful!" While thanking me over and over, he looked like a new person.

Winning the lottery could not have made me happier. For the first time in my life I experienced the truth of the saying, "It is more blessed to give than to receive." My heart was flooded with so much joy I felt that I could have floated to heaven.

I went to visit Bill the next day, but he was gone. The rental manager said she had not seen him since the previous day. I went back to the old cow pasture and he was not there either. I never saw Bill again.

That was several years ago. Did I entertain an angel unaware (Hebrews 13:2)? To this day I do not know. What I do know is that a short time later, my whole life turned around, as you will read in this book. I do not believe my life changed because I may have entertained an angel unaware. I believe it changed because of what God's Word says about taking care of the poor.

To me, giving God's way is an adventure. If I could have planned my life I would not have been able to predetermine a better one than I have experienced over the last 26 years since I became a Christian. It all started with Bill. When I met him, I had only been a Christian a short time. At that period of my life I had lost all material possessions and was living in a Sunday school room, graciously loaned to me by my pastor. I said to myself, "This Jesus fellow sure has a keen sense of humor. Not only did He take my sins away, all my money is gone as well." Of course, joking about my loss was a coping mechanism for dealing with the devastation. I knew full well that I alone was at fault for my financial problems. I had started on a financial downward spiral long before I came to Jesus.

UNEXPECTED BLESSINGS—OIL WELLS

Soon after my born-again experience and not long after my incident with Bill, my financial position began a drastic change for the good. A friend told me about an oil and gas company in Louisiana, that was selling some storage gas wells.

These wells had not produced any oil or gas for more than 15 years. They were only used as an underground storage reservoir for stockpiling production from other wells in the area. When more gas was needed the company would just turn a valve on and let the storage gas flow into the nearby pipeline. Each of the four wells was connected to the pipeline.

My friend worked for the company and it was his job to keep the record of the amount of storage gas in the reservoir. He told me that his company was selling the surface equipment to the highest bidder. He said, "I know that there is about $25,000 worth of gas in those storage wells because I put it in them. Some company will buy the surface equipment not knowing of the stored gas and make extra money on the project. It will be a good deal for whoever buys it."

Neither of us had enough money to bid on this package, so we contacted a bank that agreed to lend us the necessary money if we were the high bidder. We were shocked and a little apprehensive when we found out that we had submitted the high bid. This was a big venture and we were not quite sure how to proceed with the deal. Since I can attest that I knew absolutely nothing about oil and gas production, we solicited a Higher Power for directions. While we were asking for the Lord's guidance, the Lord brought Proverbs 3:9-10 to my remembrance: *Honor the LORD with your pos-*

*sessions, and with the firstfruits of all your increase; So your
barns will be filled with plenty, and your vats will overflow
with new wine* (NKJV).

I had already decided I would honor the Lord with all that
I had, even though at that time I did not have much. Since
Proverbs promised abundance if we honored the Lord, we
took it as a guarantee from Him, and it gave us the boldness
to go ahead with the deal by faith. We closed on the property and immediately pledged the first $25,000 from that
project to the work of the Lord. We thought that the $25,000
from the sale of the storage gas would be all the profit we
would make; it would be our first fruit.

The cost of drilling one gas well at that time was about
$250,000 and that is with no guarantee of production. We
bought the four wells ($1,000,000 value) for our bid of
$50,000. All we had to do to start production was to open the
four valves, one from each well, and let the gas and oil flow.
This was the beginning of miracles for us in this venture.

In a short period we produced $25,000 worth of gas and
paid the faith pledge as we had promised to do. A portion of
the $25,000 went to the support of missionaries and the
remainder went for feeding the poor. From what we had
seen in the Word, this was a good way to honor the Lord
with our possessions.

Let me emphasize here that this pledge was an *offering*,
not a *tithe*. It could not have been a tithe. Since we had no
concept of how much money we were going to make, there
was no way to know what one-tenth would have been. We
genuinely believed that all we would ever make on the deal
was about $25,000.

We were sure, as was everyone who had any knowledge
about these wells, that they would be depleted quickly. To all
of our amazement, however, they kept producing oil and gas!
The local geologist said that his information indicated that
there was no production in the area. Yet, our wells continued

to produce.

Soon, other large oil companies leased land and drilled all around us, but they only hit dry holes. We were reminded of the story of the widow in the Bible who gave her last bit of substance to the man of God. She thought it was her last bit of goods, but the barrel continued to be replenished (1 Kings 17). We assumed that our wells would soon dry up, but they kept producing. Six months passed and the wells were still producing. Now we were making profit big time. We were able to give even more to the work of the Lord. The more we gave the more the wells produced.

My partner and I now found ourselves in a real dilemma; all this extra money created an income tax problem. So we incorporated our company and set up a retirement plan for our families. We held board of directors meetings in Colorado, Hawaii and Europe.

Now, remember that our first pledge was not a tithe because we had no idea how much would be produced. Ten percent of nothing is nothing. Since nothing is all we had when we made the pledge, it could not have been a tithe. Our pledge was a *faith offering*. We were giving by faith based on Proverbs 3:9-10. Please note that this portion of scripture is not part of the Law. Neither is it a tithe. *First fruit giving* is strictly giving because of our love for the Lord and a faith that He will bless. It is a free-will offering for the sake of honoring God with our possessions. At the beginning of the harvest there is no way to know what the total yield will be, so a tithe cannot be given at the beginning of the harvest. Proverbs 3:9-10 is talking about voluntarily partnering with God. We were saying that we believed God's Word.

One year passed and the gas wells were still producing. Five years passed and they continued to produce. Ten years later we were still getting a monthly check from these so-called "dry holes." The people familiar with the area knew of the story. We told both them and the geologist that God was directing the fruit of the ground (the oil) to us. Large oil companies in the area inquired about our procedures and methods to keep the production flowing. They thought we had some secret method of extracting petroleum from depleted oil wells. We did. Our "secret method" was found in God's Word!

Eleven years after this miracle started I received a call from the president of a large oil company inquiring about the possibility of purchasing our production. The wells continued to produce and we continued to give. By that time we had collected almost $2 million from those dry holes! (I wonder how long the widow's barrel kept producing?)

After checking with my CPA I learned that we should not sell the production for another eleven months for income tax reasons. I called the executive of the company and told him that we could accept a contract on the wells, but the closing date had to be eleven months later. He was pleased with the deal. Eleven months later he closed on the property for the same amount that we had originally paid. This large gas company, with many experts in petroleum production knew a lot more about the possibilities of these wells than either my partner or myself. Our wells had top-hole pressures, bottom-hole pressures, well logs, and all the other items a professional would look for in a productive well. A few days after the purchase was completed I received another phone call from the president of the company who had bought the production. He said, "What did you do to make the wells produce? As soon as we bought the production from you the wells stopped producing." Needless to say I was embarrassed and told him that I would refund his money. He said, "No, we have investors who have covered the loss." In other words, it appears that he had sold more than enough ownership to investors to make money on the deal. Although I was willing to return the money, he indicated he did not feel cheated.

Many who observed this continuous miracle-in-play for

eleven years and then witnessed the production die as soon as the ownership changed hands, agreed that God's fulfillment of the guarantee in His Word was the secret of this amazing success. Acts 10:1-4 talks about a man named Cornelius who was a devout man, generous, and devoted to God. He honored the Lord with his substance (he gave to the poor), and, he was a man of prayer. One day an angel appeared to Cornelius and said, *Your prayers and your alms have come up for a memorial before God* (Acts 10:4, *NKJV*). This verse speaks of how highly God esteems giving to the poor. He will memorialize this type of generosity throughout eternity.

Now, the purpose of telling this stories is not to say you will become an oil tycoon if you give to the poor. The purpose is to ask you a question. Would you rather give God's way and have your generosity become a memorial in heaven, or hoard your finances out of selfishness or ignorance of the principle of giving? God's Word records over 7,000 promises related to giving. However, it is our responsibility as believers to rightly divide the Word of truth (2 Timothy 2:15). We must learn the truth about giving. We must not be gullible and believe everything we hear. There was a group of believers called Bereans who were commemorated in the Book of Acts. The Bereans searched out the Scriptures to ensure what they were taught was the truth. *Now the Bereans were of more noble character than the Thessalonians, for they received the message with great eagerness and examined the Scriptures every day to see if what Paul said was true* (Acts 17:11, *NIV*).

We have a great responsibility, but we also have a great reward for our faithfulness. My whole purpose for writing this book is so that God's people will be blessed, the local church will be blessed, the universal church will be blessed, and the ministers will be blessed as well.

I have several more personal testimonies (miracles)

throughout this book to share with you. I only share them to let you know that the Lord will do the same for you. He does not honor individuals, He honors His Word!

Fasten your seat belts and let's take a journey through the Bible on the subject of tithes and giving. God wants us to achieve financial success, but we must give God's way, not man's way.

FAITH GIVING

Faith giving may mean different things to different people depending on what they have been taught. Let me define what I mean. Faith giving is giving either money or possessions to another while trusting that God will guide us as to where to give, and that He will fulfill His part of the promise after we have met the conditions. Faith giving is essentially giving by faith, believing God to provide the gift, direct where to give the gift, and then bless the giver according to His Word. We read in 2 Corinthians 9:6-8, *He who sows sparingly will also reap sparingly, and he who sows bountifully will also reap bountifully. So let each one give as he purposes in his heart, not grudgingly or of necessity; for God loves a cheerful giver. And God is able to make all grace abound toward you, that you, always having all sufficiency in all things, may have an abundance for every good work (NKJV).* The conditions of this promise are as follows: 1) one reaps in proportion to what he sows, 2) he must determine in his heart what he wants to give, 3) he must give cheerfully, without resentment. The results of this promise are: 1) that God will enable us to *always* have more than enough, so that, 2) we may have an *abundance* to give to *every* good work in the future. The conditions are our part. The results are God's part.

When I discuss faith giving, I am *not* talking about giving money to receive more money. I am talking about giving money to the work of the Lord in obedience to His Word. I am also talking about the benefits of such giving because God guarantees certain blessings to the giver. I have both experienced and witnessed these benefits first-hand and will share several more testimonials to increase your faith. The purpose of these testimonials is not to get you thinking *my* way, but to direct you to giving *God's* way. As Christians, we need to understand God's guidelines when it comes to giving to the poor, the fatherless, and the widow. If we were obedient in giving God's way, there would be more than enough finances to support the local church, the local pastors, church expansion programs, and missionaries. The problem is that many have ignored the poor and forfeited the blessings that God promises.

CHAPTER TWO

Prosperity Preaching – Dangerous Deception

It is imperative that we as Christians should take a long, hard look at the Bible to obtain true, godly guidelines for giving. Too often, the victims of erroneous preaching are sincere yet gullible Christians who are often elderly and living below the poverty level. The promise of more money in return for one's giving is an easy trap for those who struggle to make ends meet. It is as seductive as gambling. The ministers even suggest that these unwitting individuals put their contribution on credit cards. These actions are wrong. True Christians condemn such acts, but what we need to realize is that those fraudulent ministers represent *us* to the rest of the world. No wonder religion is often viewed by many as a fraud! True believers know that Christianity is legitimate and that supporting Christian efforts is proper, beneficial, wholesome, and godly. Yet, how can we explain true biblical guidelines for giving if we do not understand them ourselves? Knowledge is the key. It behooves us to search the Scriptures to clarify this sensitive issue; giving away our hard-earned money! I wish the lady in the following story had done just that before she fell for the trap.

The front page headline of the Sunday, January 10, 1999, edition of the *Fort Worth Star Telegram* read "Ministry's 'prosperity preaching' is questioned." The article said, "Critics say TV evangelist has left woman broke, and homeless." The article reported that one of the contributors, a 62-year old lady supplied almost $15,000 to the ministry before finding herself broke and homeless. The Texas minister used part of the money to buy himself a new Corvette. The lady received a thank-you note that said, "GREAT BIG THANK YOU ... for blessing my socks off for my birthday!" Another letter said, "I love my Corvette. This has been the BEST Birthday of My Life!! ... 100-fold back to you too." A Christian watchdog group estimates that this minister collects $6–$8 million a year by milking sincere Christians of their money.

SELLING THE ANOINTING?

The following letters to the editor appeared in *Charisma* magazine. It is obvious by these letters and others that most Christians are disgusted with those who prostitute the Word of God.

> *I attended a meeting at which a minister told the congregation he would prophesy over anyone wanting a prophecy if they were willing to pay $100 for it. This immediately turned me off. Since then I continually get mail from this minister, asking for $100 to $400 so he can give me my prophecy from God. I throw the letters in the trash. People need to be warned about this.* (Page 8, *Charisma & Christian Life,* magazine, December 2001, Letters, name withheld).

> *I was disappointed in your feature on preachers who try to sell God's blessings ("Is the Anointing*

for sale?" by B. Courtney McBath, October). It was not strong enough. The issue has reached such epidemic proportions that the average person in the Nigerian church doesn't know how to pray for something without tying a "seed" to it.

I've sat in services nauseated because the man up front was telling people they had to bring a seed before he could pray for them. Most of us can't name great missionaries, theologians or reformers, but we know prosperity preachers. We don't know the promises of eternity, but we know verses on prosperity. Everything we learned was from the American church. Help us, Charisma. We are becoming bankrupt of the anointing. Please speak out. (Page 10, *Charisma & Christian Life,* magazine, January 2002, name withheld, Warri, Nigeria).

We need to meet needs, not to get back. We need to give with right motives. It is sad that some will give and not receive the promised return because they heard the voice of the speaker, not the Holy Spirit. Some may be hurt and leave God and the church because of this. (Page 10, *Charisma & Christian Life,* magazine, January 2002, Vestava A. Robberson, Reedley, California).

The above responses clearly indicate that sincere Christians are sick and tired of the shenanigans presented by some prosperity preachers. Thank goodness that the Holy Spirit allows genuine Christians to see through the disorder that originates from some pulpits.

A while back I attempted to witness to a Jewish fellow who I had met at a business meeting. He told me that he had a Christian friend who was very well known in the healing ministry. He said, "This preacher likes a special kind of shoe that I import from Italy. They cost $600 a pair, and he has me order 6 to 10 pairs at a time. He flies in from Florida, and I meet him at the airport with the shoes packaged so no one will know what they are." Of course, that shot down my witness. I said to myself, "Thank God all Christian leaders are not like that preacher!"

MY BARBER

I tried witnessing to my barber and he proceeded to tell me why he would not go to church. Sadly, it is because of the abuse his family endured from a so-called man of God. He said, "My single mother loved the Lord and tried to do everything commanded by her pastor. We were on food stamps and it was all my mother could do to feed her family. We barely had enough to eat. The pastor would pass the tithing plate around each Sunday. He would count the tithes right there on the spot. If the amount in the plate fell short of what he expected he would blast his faithful few for robbing God of tithes and offerings. Sometimes he would pass the tithing plate three or four times and ridicule the members each time for not giving enough to God." My barber told me how this pastor accepted all the tithes as his personal income and he taught his congregation it was their responsibility to take care of him. He told me, "The pastor bought a new Lincoln each year while my single, struggling mom and our family walked." He said, "On several occasions I saw my mother pull her last dollar out of her purse to obey the command of her pastor. All the while she knew that her children would do without because of her giving. After I got older I realized what this scamp was doing to my family. I do not want any part of him or his church." I will let you judge for yourself the danger of that type of tithing.

The sad part of this story is that there are scores of such dubious ministers who eagerly take advantage of sincere

Christians. These fiery preachers weave stories of special blessings from God in response for giving money to their ministries. They say something like, "If you send God a check today you will be blessed up to 100-fold." It works. Thousands of dollars roll in each week, and the preachers are the ones who are blessed. It has always been interesting to me that the scoundrel will say, "Give your money to God." Then he will provide his own address as if it were where God receives His mail!

TURNING FROM TRADITION

Writing this book has been interesting, challenging, and informative. What I have learned has altered my understanding of the guidelines for New Testament giving and as a result, has changed my life. I feel like I have discovered long-lost jewels buried deep beneath the sea on a sunken treasure ship. I will be forever grateful for this personal revelation of the Scriptures. Passing the information along, however, has not been so exciting. To be honest, it is very frightening because I am challenging a deeply rooted tradition in the Church establishment today. Jesus told the Pharisees, ...*Thus you nullify the word of God for the sake of your tradition* (Matthew 15:6, *NIV*). I press forward, with deep respect for the Word of God, and am willing to accept responsibility for my position against traditions of man.

Very few historical figures are as controversial as Martin Luther, the Catholic priest who in 1517, impacted the entire Church world with the astonishing insight contained in a simple passage of Scripture, *For I am not ashamed of the gospel of Christ: for it is the power of God to salvation for everyone that believeth; for the Jew first, and also for the Greek. For therein is the righteousness of God revealed from faith to faith: as it is written, The just shall live by faith* (Romans 1:16-17). Luther's supporters hailed him as a Protestant hero, a freedom fighter, and a wise and insightful church leader. His detractors branded him a heretic, an apostate, and a profane ecclesiastical terrorist.

Luther, himself, marveled that a straightforward stand of conscience turned him into one of the most talked about people of his time. Yet, that simple Christian and his simple stand of conscience started an ecclesiastical shockwave that changed the course of Christian history.

Luther arrived at the Diet of Worms conference as part of a triumphal procession. The emperor and church officials expected him to recant his thesis while at this conference. Luthers' books were placed on a table. He was then asked if they were his works and whether he wanted to recant any of the information. Luther requested time to think over his reply and the next day he answered with the well-known speech:

> *Unless I am convicted by Scripture and plain reason—I do not accept the authority of the popes and councils, for they have contradicted each other—my conscience is captive to the Word of God. I cannot and I will not recant anything for to go against conscience is neither right nor safe. Here I stand. I cannot do otherwise. God help me, Amen!*

Challenges of tradition may be positive, as Martin Luther established. Millions have received the truth about the grace of God because of the stand he took. Nuggets of biblical truth has been revealed to millions in the last few decades that heretofore were considered heresy. Yet, these truths were in the Bible all the while. They had either been overlooked or disregarded. So it is with the method of giving, recorded in the Bible, for New Testament Christians. It appears that many Christian organizations have moved back under the Law to establish giving requirements for their members. Inspired by Luther's stance, I drew a line in the sand and take my stand for Bible truth regarding New Testament giving.

It was not my choice to write this book. I felt impressed to compile this study for a long time, but I was afraid that some might be offended by its controversial contents even though it presents truth. My fear was obliterated when the Lord reminded me that He had spared my life so many times, especially when I was a Navy fighter pilot. This very dangerous profession claimed the lives of many of my friends who flew supersonic Navy Fighters aboard aircraft carriers. I had no choice but to obey my Savior on this project. So fasten your seat belts and hang on for an interesting flight through the Scriptures.

POVERTY PREACHING

There was a time in recent church history where believers were not taught that God wanted to bless them financially. God tried to send the truth by calling preachers who would dare preach that He wanted to bless and prosper His people. This was no easy task because for a long time poverty had been preached as though it were a badge of spirituality. The poverty message, whether subtle or blatant, was "God is not pleased with you if you have money." No true Christian wants to displease God so the majority of the people bought it. Many believed that if they wanted to serve God whole-heartedly, they could not prosper. In other words, wealth and spirituality were not compatible terms.

To turn the tide of this false teaching and break the yoke of poverty, God raised up preachers who would dare preach that good, honest, sincere Christians do not have to be poor. Reverend Kenneth E. Hagin, who is often called the father of the faith movement, out of which sprang the prosperity message, was one of them. Through the testimony of his own miraculous healing from an incurable, terminal disease,

Hagin discovered that God did not want His people to live impotent lives in bondage to sickness and poverty. Among other truths, he preached healing, victory, and prosperity, messages that were foreign to many because of the religious spirits that had held them in bondage.

Hagin's ministry is tried and true. For over sixty years he has maintained his integrity and anointing and he is well respected throughout the world for his balanced teaching. In one of his most recent books, entitled *The Midas Touch, A Balanced Approach to Biblical Prosperity*, (Faith Library Publications, Tulsa, OK, 2000), Hagin explains how in the beginning, so much poverty had been preached that much of the church establishment in America was extreme in their belief. You could not convince them that they could be prosperous and godly at the same time. The Bible does warn us that one cannot serve God and money (Matthew 6:24). The solution would be for one's money to serve the purposes of God rather than his greediness and/or selfishness. The Bible also states that the love of money is the root of all evil (1 Timothy 6:10). These warnings, however, do not mean that poverty is a sign of a God-fearing, God-loving, holy Christian!

Many of God's saints in the Old Testament were very wealthy people, and for the most part their wealth did not interfere with their relationship with God. We read that, *The weight of gold that Solomon received yearly was 666 talents, not including the revenues from merchants and traders and from all the Arabian kings and the governors of the land ... King Solomon was greater in riches and wisdom than all the kings of the earth* (1 Kings 10:14-23, *NIV*). The value of the 666 talents of gold on today's market would exceed $240,000,000. We must conclude that God loves to bless His people.

Since poverty preaching had been extreme, these prosperity preachers, as they came to be known, had to be extreme as well. Unfortunately, many of these sincere ministers made the same mistake their predecessors made. They left the main road of truth and ended up in the opposite ditch, misusing the Scriptures, preaching heresy and leading people astray. The Bible warns that such people, ... *imagine that godliness or righteousness is a source of profit [a money-making business, a means of livelihood]. From such withdraw* (1 Timothy 6:5, *Amplified Bible*).

So, we see that the Bible contains stern warnings about money, but these warnings are not intended to keep the Christians poor. They are intended to keep them pure, that is, pure from the *love of money*. There is a difference. People who have no money at all can sin through the *love of* money, such as stealing, coveting, or having excessive debt.

Hagin explained how the key to freedom is balance. Truth must be pursued in a balanced, loving way that avoids extremism, legalism, and dogmatism; for these only serve to put people in bondage. In dealing with this issue, Hagin quoted a friend of his, Reverend Bob Buess. I elected to include this quote because I believe it states well the value of balance. Buess stated:

> *A few years ago I was interested in a certain teaching, so I began to pursue the Word of God to find more on this subject. I believed the Bible from cover to cover, but I allowed myself to disregard certain scriptures. I blanked out certain truths. My mind became completely indifferent to certain verses in the Word.*
>
> *My new dogma was no different from the old, but I began to defend my new doctrine. It was, in a subtle way, becoming a god that I had to defend and protect. I was not an unusual case. It's easy for Christians to pursue a thought that the Holy Spirit aroused in them as they studied the Scriptures. In*

their excitement, they set out to explore the Word of God to see what could be found. When they find a few scriptures to support this newfound idea, they soon can be running madly through the Bible trying to prove their theory.

Dogmatism begins to set in. Without fully realizing what they are doing, these people jump verses, throw out some, and ignore others to prove their point ....

People driven by this cause rush madly on in a pursuit of new arguments to promote their theory. As time passes they become harsh.

The purpose of this book is ... a call to take seriously James 3:1 that condemns the teacher who dogmatically rushes ahead without balance in his teaching.

The Apostle Paul wrote a letter to the Galatian Christians who were leaving the simplicity of the gospel and reverting to rules and regulations. That Galatian spirit is working in the Body of Christ today, causing some believers to be legalistic in their approach to the Word and to be hard and dogmatic in dealing with truth and with people (p. 185-186, *The Midas Touch, A Balanced Approach to Biblical Prosperity*).

There is some truth to the prosperity message, but there are also some abuses. Hagin told about a minister who was a part of the healing revival of the 1940s and 1950s. This gifted preacher knew how to build people's faith to receive healing and miracles from the Lord. People were getting out of wheelchairs and receiving the restoration of their hearing or sight. Oftentimes the services would be high with excitement as the people began to experience the genuine miraculous power of God. Then suddenly, when the people were on an emotional high, the preacher would take advantage of the situation and say, "We're not going to pass the offering plate again, but if you have a special gift, you can bring it down to me here at the front. Don't come unless you're going to bring at least $50!"

Hagin said, "I watched as people almost ran over each other hurrying down to give him their $50. My spirit was grieved as I saw what was happening. Those people were not giving because they had purposed in their heart to help the Gospel go forth or to see other people healed. I don't believe they were giving it any thought or prayerful consideration at all. Rather, they were caught up in the emotional outburst. Wanting to be part of the thrill and excitement of the moment, they were manipulated and exploited by this minister" (p. 105-106, *The Midas Touch, A Balanced Approach to Biblical Prosperity*).

In *The Midas Touch*, Hagin provides some rational guidelines for giving. He says, "Believers should look for organizations to support that are productive for the Kingdom of God, ministries that are actively contributing to the preaching of the Gospel and the expansion of the Church."

Stephen Arterburn, the founder and chairman of New Life Clinics (a Christian mental health treatment program), a licensed minister and a best-selling author of over two dozen books, wrote an intriguing book entitled *Toxic Faith* (WaterBrook Press, a division of *Random House, Inc.*, copyright 1991, 2001). In it, he related several stories of all types of religious extremism, many of which have caused sincere Christians to become so depressed that they have become suicidal and must be hospitalized. He says, "In each experience, whether extreme or closer to the norm, faith becomes toxic when individuals use God or religion for profit, power, pleasure, and/or prestige. These four preoccupations are the foundation of any addiction; and they must be excised from faith. Each time they are allowed to distort or minimize true faith, people are hurt, some are killed, and many are left to suffer alone."

Arterburn deals with twenty-one beliefs of a toxic faith. I will only address the two which are related to money: These toxic beliefs are: 1) *Material blessings are a sign of spiritual strength,* and 2) *The more money I give to God, the more money He will give to me* (p. 44-46). Although a rational person would immediately recognize the first belief as false, due to extreme prosperity preaching, many have fallen for the second one. Often the purpose of this preaching is not to help Christians to prosper, but to provide profit, power, pleasure, and/or prestige for the preachers. We must be spiritually keen enough not to be taken in by such preaching.

POWERFUL PULPIT/COCKPIT

I feel a deep responsibility to point out errors in church teaching, not only with the church members, but also with the church leadership. Discovering error and correcting it is a key to survival for pilots as well as for their crew and passengers. Several airline crashes were attributed to the fact that Captains would not listen to, or take friendly professional advice from their crewmembers. Because of this "mightier than thou" attitude many needless crashes have occurred. In one disaster, the Captain told his co-pilot and his flight engineer to keep their mouth shut about the operation of the airplane. He said, "I am the Captain, I run the ship, and I do not need help from anyone." The crew still tried to tell him that they were running out of fuel, but he would not listen. Because of his attitude they all died when the plane crashed, due to fuel starvation, only a few miles short of the runway! The recovered voice recorder told the story too late to correct the problem.

When error is discovered, all hands are responsible to bring it to the attention of those in the chain of command. If a valid point is noted, a responsible leader should make the necessary changes in order to correct a perilous situation. As Captain with a major airline, and as president of several corporations, I cherish input from all individuals on my team. Therefore, I am only trying to inform, to accentuate Bible truth about proper New Testament giving procedures. Some may say that it is not my responsibility to challenge how others give and receive. The Holy Ghost will lead me and guide me to all truth. Some listen to Him, some do not!

The media and public ministry, such as the pulpit of a local church, are powerful tools with the ability to sway people for either good or evil. They can be a blessing or a curse. There are many trustworthy ministries using the media for the good of mankind, as you will read at the end of this book. Unfortunately, however, there are many whom I call reprobates who take advantage of the naive and are only concerned with building their personal wealth. Even my own 90 year-old mother has written checks to media ministries just because they made an appeal and promised that those who gave would receive a special financial blessing. More often than not, these are bogus promises that will never materialize because they are not truly based on God's Word.

It is important that we know who is worthy of our support and who is not. I know of one pastor who checks his congregations' giving records because he claims that their disobedience to tithe (obey the Law) is a reflection of a rebellious heart. Misusing the scripture in Proverbs 27:23, he says that God requires him to know the state of his flock. This is an invasion of privacy. Giving is a very personal and private matter. This pastor may mean well, but he is wrong. He is preoccupied with performance. The Apostle Paul rebuked the church at Galatia for reverting back into the Law. Galatians 3:1-3: *You foolish Galatians! Who has bewitched you? Before your very eyes Jesus Christ was clearly portrayed as crucified. I would like to learn just one thing from you: Did you receive the Spirit by observing the law, or by believing what you heard? Are you so foolish? After beginning with the Spirit, are you now trying to attain your goal by human effort?* (*NIV*). Just as with every other area of our lives, our giving must come under the control of the Holy Spirit.

God spoke through the prophet Jeremiah about those ministers who have their own profit, power, pleasure, and/or prestige at heart. In Jeremiah 5:26-31, He said, *"Among my people are wicked men who lie in wait like men who snare birds and like those who set traps to catch men. Like cages full of birds, their houses are full of deceit; they have become rich and powerful and have grown fat and sleek. Their evil deeds have no limit; they do not plead the case of the fatherless to win it, they do not defend the rights of the poor. Should I not punish them for this?" declares the LORD. "Should I not avenge myself on such a nation as this? A horrible and shocking thing has happened in the land: The prophets prophesy lies, the priests rule by their own authority, and my people love it this way. But what will you do in the end?"* (*NIV*).

God holds us accountable for our finances. This includes our giving; how much we give and to whom we give it. To blindly give money to a minister (who promises God will give more back) and say that what he does with it is between him and God is to be a reckless and irresponsible steward of ones money. It is also reckless and irresponsible stewardship of ones free will. We are free to believe what we will. We can believe the truth, or we can believe a lie.

When Christ asks us at the judgment seat what we did with our resources, it will not be good enough to say, "I obeyed the preacher." He will want to know if we obeyed Him. If not, why not? I believe He is asking you a question today. Would you like your money to possibly be used to support the lavish lifestyle of some scoundrel, or would you want it to go up as a memorial before God for helping the needy as recorded in Acts Chapter 10? Would you want your money to be wasted by someone who is reckless and careless? Of course not! If you want to receive God's guarantees then you must ensure that your giving is in accordance with the Word of God, and not in accordance with the commands of a greedy man or a man who himself might be a poor financial steward.

God's Word is clear on the subject of giving as we read in Luke Chapter 8. The Lord said, *Plant your seeds into good ground.* Our responsibility is to locate the *good ground* and plant good seed into it. God does not make mistakes, but man makes many. This is why we must know and understand the Lord's financial insurance, written to all mankind, on how to give. *His* plan will not fail. God's Word guarantees financial blessing for remembering the poor, the widow, and the fatherless. It does not guarantee financial blessing for supporting the lavish lifestyles of greedy ministers. We must be aware of the danger of wrong prosperity preaching so that we may be good stewards of the finances with which God has entrusted us and achieve true financial success God's way!

*Note: To help you discern between a healthy, sound ministry and one that is not worthy of your financial support, I have included some guidelines at the back of this report in Appendix I entitled **How to Judge a Healthy, Sound Ministry**.

CHAPTER THREE

Giving or Tithing?

Pressuring unsuspecting believers to give monetary offerings and then using some or all of the contributions to pad their pockets, is a method by which greedy, out-of-control preachers violate the trust, generosity, and spiritual devotion of believers today. Teaching that tithing is the only way a believer can come under the financial blessing and protection of God is another method of deception. Neither of these methods line up with the Word of God. Faulty prosperity preaching is taught from the standpoint that if Christians would faithfully tithe they would be blessed by God and would achieve financial success. While most pastors probably mean well, they are only teaching what they have been taught. They have not searched the Scriptures for themselves to see if tithing is an authentic New Testament practice. Thus they are neglectful shepherds. They have not applied themselves to learning the truth, nor have they committed themselves to teaching the truth to their congregations.

I do not wish to be harsh with these men of God. There could be many reasons why these doctrines are taught in churches, some of which are not intended to abuse anyone. These could be genuine mistakes inherited from previous un-informed generations. However, a good motive does not excuse us from seeking good doctrine.

Jesus rebuked the shepherds of His day because they taught only tradition, *Full well ye reject the commandment of God, that ye may keep your own traditions* (Mark 7:9). In verse 13, He said that their practice to do so was, *Making the Word of God of none effect through your tradition, which ye have delivered and many such things you do.* They made the Word of God null and void by their traditions.

Having said this, it is not enough to blame the preachers. It is the responsibility of each believer to search the Scriptures to find the truth. Learning and continuing in the truth is how we find freedom in Christ (John 8:31-32). Our freedom comes from Christ; it does not come from the pastor or the evangelist. The truth sets us free. Jesus said that He is the Truth (John 14:6). He sent the Holy Spirit to convey to us the truth (John 16:13). The Holy Spirit does this both corporately and individually for the purpose of making us free. *Now the Lord is the Spirit; and where the Spirit of the Lord is, there is liberty* (2 Corinthians 3:17, NKJV). The purpose of seeking and finding the truth is to be free in Christ. This is the reason Jesus came to Earth, to free us from the bondage of sin, the power of Satan, and the ravages of our own disobedience (1 John 3:8). Jesus has done His part. We must do ours. We cannot depend on the preachers to be totally without error. We must be like the Bereans previously discussed in Chapter 1. We must examine *the Scriptures every day to see if what* we hear is *true* (Acts 17:11, NIV).

Giving to the poor is the subject that launched me into this meticulous study. I was researching scriptures regarding helping the needy, and that investigation directed me to the subject of tithing. I was shocked at what I discovered. *Surely, this was just a misunderstanding on my part*, I thought. However, the more I investigated God's Word and the more I learned about the subject of tithing, the more I realized that I had been deceived. I felt violated. Not only had I been misinformed, but millions of others have been misinformed as well.

I honestly do not believe that the intention of our local church leadership is to defraud anyone. I do believe, however, that they were handed down the tradition of tithing and accepted it without question. This practice has lead to error. A few years ago a friend tried in vain to advise me that tithing was not a New Testament command. I would have no part of his conversation. I knew he was wrong. My spiritual leaders had taught me otherwise! In other words, I let the command of man overrule the instructions of God. Tradition hides truth. Ritual can destroy right.

After many hours of research, after deliberating with many Bible scholars, and more importantly, after much prayer, I was shocked beyond belief to find out that tithing is not a New Testament command! I was even more shocked to learn where this false teaching for New Testament churches originated (as discussed in Chapter 11). I have prayed the following prayer many times, "Lord, if it is Your will for me to continue this study, then reveal more information on this subject to me." Without exception, after each prayer, I would find additional information proving that tithing is not a New Testament requirement. Of course, the Bible is the ultimate source for accurate information. I discovered many excellent reports on tithing while searching the Internet. And I found numerous books written on this subject. Many sincere pastors who have graduated from some of the nations most respected Bible seminaries agree that the directive of tithing was part of the Law and is not a requirement for Christians today. I was offended and upset when I realized that I had been misinformed about tithing.

In Luke Chapter 18 Jesus taught about two men—one of them tithed, and one did not. *Two men went up to the temple to pray, one a Pharisee and the other a tax collector. The*

Pharisee stood and prayed thus with himself, God, I thank You that I am not like other men—extortioners, unjust, adulterers, or even as this tax collector. I fast twice a week; <u>I give tithes of all that I possess.</u> And the tax collector, standing afar off, would not so much as raise his eyes to heaven, but beat his breast, saying, God, be merciful to me a sinner! I tell you, this man went down to his house justified rather than the other ... (Luke 18:10-12, *NIV*). It does not take a rocket scientist to see which one pleased Jesus.

SITUATIONAL AWARENESS

I am sure you are like me in that you want to please Jesus. If tithing pleased Him, we would surely want to be faithful tithe payers. On the other hand, what if tithing is not pleasing to Him? If we have a situation in the church that needs correcting, shouldn't we be willing and eager to correct it? Situational Awareness is a buzz phrase that defines the evaluation of personnel and/or organizations. It is a measure to indicate achievements and failures, effectiveness and ineffectiveness. The purpose of Situational Awareness is to locate areas of weakness and then to recommend guidelines for improvement.

In starting our search throughout the Scriptures for the truth concerning tithing, let us consider the following Situational Awareness statements. Further into the study, we will address each one of these statements.

TWENTY SEVEN REASONS OR CONSIDERATIONS FOR NOT TITHING

1. There was no command to tithe before, or after the Law.
2. Did Adam and Eve, Job, Noah or Joseph tithe?
3. Why did God reject Cain's gift?
4. Tithing is not commanded in the Ten Com-

mandments.

5. The tithe was never money; it was always agricultural products.
6. Tithes are to be eaten.
7. Tithes are to go into the storehouse.
8. Under the Law one could redeem his tithes.
9. Only a tenth of the tithe went to the priest.
10. Every three years the tithe went to the needy.
11. Every seven years there was no tithe.
12. The people paid a tithe to themselves.
13. Tithes were for the Levites, widows, aliens and fatherless.
14. All priests were Levites, but not all Levites were priests.
15. The Law tolerated many wives, concubines, sacrifices, and tithes. (The implication here is if we teach one of these practices—why not all?)
16. Who is robbing God of tithes and offerings?
17. Jesus did not tithe, nor did He accept tithes.
18. The New Testament Church did not tithe.
19. The New Testament command concerning giving: *Every man as he purposeth.*
20. Since the New Testament salvation plan is superior to the Old Testament salvation plan, we can conclude that the New Testament giving plan is superior to the Old Testament giving plan. We have a better covenant with better promises. Which plan should we follow?
21. God honors acceptable gifts and rejects unacceptable gifts.
22. The Pope reinstated tithing at the Council of Macon in 585 A.D.
23. Where do your tithes go?

24. Should we support the church and the ministry? Absolutely! But not by the Old Testament Law of tithing.
25. Present day priests, pastors, and preachers are not restricted from owning land, as were their counterparts in the Old Testament.
26. Why are not all who tithe wealthy?
27. Are you blessed financially for tithing, or for giving to the poor?

There are a lot more than 27 reasons why New Testament Christians should not tithe, but these should be sufficient for this study.

IS GIVING IMPORTANT?

The purpose of this study is to determine the New Testament directives for giving. It is not to say that we should give *less* if tithing is not a New Testament practice. It is to say that when it comes to the business of God, we must be generous. What better cause could there be than God's cause?

I do not oppose giving to the church, paying the ministers, or building places of worship, as long as the giving is in compliance with the Bible. Scriptural based giving brings God's guarantees with it. On the other hand, the reason so many have not been blessed is because they have given in response to the command of man instead of the command of God. You will read in this book about those who gave God's way and were blessed, not only spiritually, but financially as well. You will also read about some who gave out of manipulation, coercion, or deception, and received nothing but heartache and even destitution for their generosity.

To emphasize how important giving is in God's estimation, let me use the following comparisons. We find 215 scriptures in the New Testament on the subject of prayer, so we know that the Lord expects us to pray. We find 218 scriptures on praise in the New Testament, so we are assured and encouraged to lift up praises to our Lord. Do you know how many times the New Testament mentions giving? 2,088! There are almost ten times as many references to giving as there are to praying or praising. WOW! God clearly wants more than lip service from us. Could it be that no matter how much we pray or praise God, we should be giving ten times more? We must give, then give some more, and then find more ways to give to His cause. God loves a cheerful giver and will bless all of our gestures of generosity. Giving to God is the thermometer that indicates our love for Him. Giving a gift (freely) sure sounds better than paying (tithes) a debt. If we all gave according to God's directive, the pastors would be paid, the church's needs would be met, the missionaries would be adequately supported, and the poor and fatherless would be cared for as well.

Surely you have heard the saying, "I have been rich and I have been poor. Rich is better." I would like to say that I have tithed, and I have given, and giving is better! Why? Since tithing is not commanded after the cross, there is no guarantee for financial blessing for paying tithes. I have been blessed more since I stopped tithing and started giving God's way. Man has reinvented the Old Testament commands for tithing, but man is not able to guarantee the blessings for such actions. Therefore, many sincere Christians who tithe are deceived. They are promised blessings that may or may not materialize, and the unfortunate part of this story is the enormous number of us who do not know the difference.

Many in the clergy are not aware of the tithing error. They have faithfully preached what they have been taught, but tradition is not always truth. For example, it was once an accepted tradition to use leeches to "bleed" people to cure them of a host of diseases. Of course, this tradition caused many premature deaths. Ultimately, truth was discovered, the error was corrected, and many lives were saved. I challenge you to search for truth and let go of your tradition if you discover what I say to be true. Truth will produce blessings for us all: for the church, the pastor, and the giver. Tithing is analyzed in depth later in this study.

God is eager to bless His people financially and every word in His book is true. Many who are in poverty and financial difficulty today <u>could be</u> wealthy if they would only obey God's Word on the subject of giving.

THE CORRECT ATTITUDE ABOUT MONEY

Money is more than paper with pictures of dead presidents. Money is the result of your labors; it is the return of your time, your sweat, your energy, and your mental abilities. With it, you bargain and exchange for goods and services, you express your love for your family, and you express your love for God by giving to Him.

Giving intrigues God. A giving heart draws favor from God. Giving to God is your private expression that He is important to you. Giving indicates that you have faith in Him. Your giving reveals where your heart is. Giving reveals a confident, faithful, thankful, and generous heart. God will be indebted to no man. You cannot out-give Him, so the more you give God's way, the more He will repay.

Many are quick to say that money is the root of all evil. The problem is not money but the *love* of money. Some people trust in their riches more than they trust in God. *For the love of money is the root of all evil: which while some coveted after, they have erred from the faith, and pierced themselves through with many sorrows ...Charge them that are rich in this world, that they be not highminded, nor trust in uncertain riches, but in the living God, who giveth us richly all things to enjoy; That they do good, that they be rich in good works, <u>ready to distribute</u>, willing to communicate; Laying up in store for themselves a good foundation against the time to come, that they may lay hold on eternal life* (l Timothy 6:10-

17). This scripture reveals the correct attitude about money and riches. Many of God's leaders in the Bible were wealthy. I believe one of the reasons they were memorialized in biblical history is because they used their wealth to help others. God had their stories recorded in the Scriptures as examples for us to follow today. The Bible says:

Beloved, I wish above all things that thou mayest prosper and be in health, even as thy soul prospereth (3 John 2).

And keep the charge of the LORD thy God, to walk in his ways, to keep his statutes, and his commandments ... that thou mayest prosper in all that thou doest, and whithersoever thou turnest thyself (1 Kings 2:3).

The Lord spoke a great deal about money and the problems it causes man—in fact, one-fifth of all Jesus had to say was about money. In addition to these points, God's chosen fast revolves around giving, as we read in Isaiah 58:6-7: *Is not this the fast that I have chosen? To loose the bands of wickedness, to undo the heavy burdens, and to let the oppressed go free, and that ye break every yoke? Is it not to deal thy bread to the hungry, and that thou bring the poor that are cast out to thy house? when thou seest the naked, that thou cover him; and that thou hide not thyself from thine own flesh?* Although money can be a problem it is obvious that money is important to God.

BIBLICAL GUARANTEES

The following financial guarantee is for you and your children if you obey the Lord. *Blessed is the man <u>who fears the LORD,</u> who finds great delight in his commands. <u>His children will be mighty in the land</u>; the generation of the upright* will be blessed. *Wealth and riches are in his house, and his righteousness endures forever. Even in darkness light dawns for the upright, for the gracious and compassionate and righteous man. Good will come to him who is generous and lends freely, who conducts his affairs with justice. Surely he will never be shaken; a righteous man will be remembered forever. He will have no fear of bad news; his heart is steadfast, trusting in the LORD. His heart is secure, he will have no fear; in the end he will look in triumph on his foes. He has scattered abroad his gifts to the poor, his righteousness endures forever; his horn will be lifted high in honor. The wicked man will see and be vexed, he will gnash his teeth and waste away; the longings of the wicked will come to nothing* (Psalms 112, *NIV*).

In review of the above Chapter you will find very specific actions that one can take and be guaranteed success for himself and his children. Note the phrases, *...who fears the Lord ... his children will be mighty in the land ... gracious and compassionate ... no fear of bad news ... triumph on his foes ... scattered abroad his gifts to the poor.* These trustworthy promises can be yours as well. Never let it be said that the Lord wants His people to be poor. **If God's guarantees concerning giving fail, then we have the right to question all other biblical facts, which include the virgin birth, the resurrection, and the second coming of Jesus!** We know these are true. To the same degree, we can depend on God's guarantees for giving.

Money can be a curse or a blessing. All we need to do is look around and observe those who have large sums of money without Christ. Most of these so-called lucky ones are unhappy, which shows us that a blessing from the windows of heaven can bring wealth *with* joy, but the windows of a crooked business deal, or from a Las Vegas win can bring grief. God gives riches and blessings if we only obey Him. *The living God, who giveth us richly all things to enjoy*

... (l Timothy 6:17). *The blessing of the LORD brings wealth, and he adds no trouble to it* (Proverbs 10:22, *NIV*).

One thing is for sure; the devil is bankrupt and he can never recover from his sentence. We, however, have the opportunity to increase our eternal financial status. Jesus said, *Give, and it shall be given unto you; good measure, pressed down, and shaken together, and running over, shall men give into your bosom* (Luke 6:38).

God, the possessor of all monies, is willing to entrust some to you. Job, Abraham, Isaac, Jacob, David, and Solomon were just a few of the extremely wealthy men whom God prospered. If your father were a billionaire don't you think he would want you to enjoy some of his wealth? Don't you think he would willingly share it with you? Our heavenly Father is much richer than any earthly father and He wants us to prosper. But, we must obey His Word concerning giving so He can legitimately bless us. We hold God's "wallet" in our hands. If He observes that we freely give as He directs, then He will enlarge the channel through which He sends blessings. With how much can He entrust us, $100, $1,000, $100,000, or millions? Are you a financial conduit of God's blessings? Remember that you set your limits, not God. How do you set your limits? Simply by the degree that you obey His commands. God wants us to trust Him ... Test Him ... and Prove Him and see if He will not give us more than we can contain.

WHY SHOULD WE GIVE?

God does not need your money; He only wants your obedience. Even that is for your benefit, not His. This study could end with only the above verses for assurance, but there are many more which are loaded with promises. I learned long ago that if I wanted to increase my standard of living, all I had to do was increase my standard of giving and God would increase my standard of living. *I tell you, use worldly wealth to gain friends for yourselves, so that when it is gone, you will be welcomed into eternal dwellings* (Luke 16:9, *NIV*).

One must release seeds of faith to see an increase. That is, if you give to God, He will give more back to you. Releasing says, "I believe in God." Releasing says, "Money does not control me." Releasing says, "God is more important to me than my bank account." When you release, you open the very floodgates of heaven. Remember this: *Whoever sows sparingly will also reap sparingly, and whoever sows generously will also reap generously* (2 Corinthians 9:6, *NIV*). A wise man once said, "A man there was, and they called him mad; the more he gave, the more he had" (John Bunyan, 1628–1688).

Does God need our giving, or do we need to give to Him? The following verses proclaim that God can and will make it without our little amount of giving. But can we survive financially and spiritually without giving to Him? *If I were hungry I would not tell you, for the world is mine, and all that is in it* (Psalms 50:12). What an awesome opportunity we have of investing in the productive power of God. Neither a stockbroker nor a banker can match God's guaranteed returns. Who owns the world's money? *The silver is mine, and the gold is mine, saith the LORD of hosts* (Haggai 2:8). We are only stewards for what He allows us to have. *But thou shalt remember the LORD thy God: for it is he that giveth thee power to get wealth...* (Deuteronomy 8:18).

GIVING GOD'S WAY

We must learn how to give according to God's plan. Please carefully study the following scriptures regarding giving. You may be surprised, as I was, to learn what the Bible teaches about this important subject. Please note the diverse classifications of contributions that the Lord has required from mankind in the past.

... Bring your burnt <u>offerings</u> and <u>sacrifices</u>, your <u>tithes</u> and <u>special gifts</u>, <u>what you have vowed to give</u> and your <u>freewill offerings</u>, and the <u>firstborn</u> of your herds and flocks (Deuteronomy 12:6, *NIV*).

A generous man will himself be blessed, for <u>he shares his food with the poor</u> (Proverbs 22:9, *NIV*).

<u>He who gives to the poor</u> will lack nothing, but he who closes his eyes to them receives many curses (Proverbs 28:27, *NIV*). Have we unknowingly caused ourselves to be cursed?

Jesus answered, "If you want to be perfect, go, sell your possessions <u>and give to the poor,</u> and you will have treasure in heaven. Then come, follow me" (Matthew 19:21, *NIV*). This verse will be explained in detail in a later chapter.

<u>Each man should give what he has decided in his heart to give,</u> not reluctantly or under compulsion, for God loves a cheerful giver (2 Corinthians 9:7, *NIV*).

As you can see, the Lord's Holy Book lists many types of giving. In fact, giving is the theme of the Bible. God gave His only begotten Son to redeem sinful man. The words give, gave, or given are written repeatedly throughout the Bible. In most cases this expression was used to indicate what God had given, or is willing to give to man, if we will only obey Him.

CAUTION
You will note the Lord saying in several places through-out the Bible, "Trust Me ... Test Me ... Prove Me and see if

I will not give you more than you can contain." God guarantees His programs. He is not a liar! You can count on what He promises. However, I say this with a stout CAUTION! Make sure that you are really giving God's way. Many who give are not blessed. Why? I believe it is because they have responded to the manipulation of men rather than the pure Word of God. Unfortunately, there are many crafty fund-raising gimmicks today that are disgusting to the Lord and to man as well. High-pressure, guilt-laden, emotional tactics, promoted in the name of God that have little or no biblical basis, are used to manipulate many sincere Christians. Others are misled because they have no clear understanding of the Bible concerning giving. These poor souls are generous, but their giving is in vain. They are giving to man-made programs that have no guarantees. **God's guarantees concerning giving are as trustworthy as the doctrines of the virgin birth, the resurrection, and the second coming of Jesus.** I know one sincere family (I will call them the Dawsons) who gave over $400,000 to their pastor. It was all they had. This precious couple had just become Christians and they were eager to do something great for their God (new Christians can be so gullible, even foolish. It's sad, but true). They figured, *How could we possibly go wrong giving $400,000 to God?* It sounds wonderfully generous. They had probably heard sermons about Jesus praising the woman who gave a mite. It was all she had. They wanted Jesus' approval and they desired to please Him. However, after giving their generous contribution, they lived in extreme poverty for years.

This situation bothered me for a long time. *Why was God not blessing them,* I wondered? *Does God only live up to His Word when He wants to? Is this the kind of contract that God writes? Did God deceive this family, or did man?* I knew many promises listed in the Bible on giving, yet these folks were not blessed. I wondered *why?* It really troubled me. Years later I learned why. Their gift went to support the lavish lifestyle of their spiritual leader rather than to support of the work of the Lord. The Lord did not guarantee their gift since it was not specific to any of His commands. *Whose mouths must be stopped. Who subvert whole houses, teaching things which they ought not, for filthy lucre's sake* (Titus 1:11).

What can we conclude? We have seen that God wants to bless us. We have also seen that our giving is the catalyst through which He increases our finances. We can conclude that we must be responsible in our giving. Giving just to give, or giving out of emotional appeals, or giving out of an obligation to tithe, will not prompt God to bless us unless these motives are in compliance with God's directives for the New Testament Church. In Chapter 4 we will explain God's divine insurance policy. We will discover why some are blessed and some are not blessed for giving.

CHAPTER FOUR

True Faith Giving Provides Divine Insurance

We have seen in the previous chapters that giving can be done by man's directive or by God's directive. When giving is done by God's directive, then it is done by faith and His Word ensures certain blessings for the giver. If the giving is done by man's directive, then there is no guarantee for the giver. Let me share a couple of testimonies with you to illustrate the difference.

First of all, testimonials are a common marketing tool, no matter what product, service, or idea is being advertised. Weight loss product commercials, for example, are notorious for "before" and "after" testimonies extolling the benefits of their products. The purpose of these testimonials is to sell the viewer on the idea or product. The implication is, if it worked for these folks, it will work for you, too. Prosperity preachers do the same thing. Mingled in with their preaching are true-life stories of individuals who gave money into their ministries and received large sums of money from unexpected sources. The purpose of the testimonies is to authenticate the

Word they are preaching. Or, it would be better said, to authenticate their *interpretation* of the Word they are preaching. While some of the "prosperity preaching" may be scripturally accurate, much of it is not because the preacher is often the only one who benefits from sermons on faith giving.

BIBLE INSURANCE

God has intervened in my life many times since I started on the adventure of faith giving. My testimony in Chapter One told about the miracle of the oil wells. "Here is the rest of the story," as Paul Harvey says. Because of the increase of my financial position I was offered many business deals. Most of them were not worthy of consideration. However, one friend asked me to invest in a shopping mall with him. He said, "This is a deal that won't fail. It will make us a lot of money." The fact is, the banker who was going to finance the project said, "Ron if I were not restricted by bank regulations, *I* would go into partnership with you on this mall." I told these two gentlemen that I needed to leave the office for a few moments and consider the offer. I wanted to pray about it, and I did.

I am skeptical of many who say, "God told me this, or that." But, that day I believe that I heard God say loud and clear, "No! Do not invest in this mall." So I told my associates that I did not want in on the deal. Then they promised me everything! They increased the percentage of my ownership and said that I would never have to pay one penny. They said that they just needed my financial statement to help secure the loan. Then they really put me on a guilt trip by saying, "If you do not get in the deal we will loose $250,000 earnest money." You guessed it. I gave in. I signed the note for $1.5 million dollars. Why not? They assured me, "You can't lose on a deal like this, we will make a ton of money."

We bought the property for $4.7 million. It appraised for $12 million. Our company borrowed an additional $1.5 million to remodel the mall early in the venture. The $1.5 million note had to be guaranteed by each partner and I signed that contract. We expected to make about $7 million profit on this deal in a short time. *Can't lose on a deal like that.* Or, so I thought. I was sure that I had mistaken the voice of God when the "NO" came during my prayer. *Surely, this was the devil trying to keep me out of this lucrative deal*, I thought.

The oil and gas industry took a nosedive shortly after we purchased the shopping mall. West Texas property lost value rapidly. This was during the time when asbestos in buildings was making headlines. Federal law required that this material be removed from all property and our mall was fabricated with tons of asbestos. Needless to say we could not sell the property, and the bank foreclosed. The $1.5 million was due and payable by all partners. One of my partners went back to Europe and the other one had no means to pay. I was the local target for collection. I was guilty. I had signed the note and I was responsible for the entire amount. Interest on this note exceeded $200,000 annually. My wife and I prayed profusely about this predicament. Now I was ready to listen to and obey the Lord. This was my "belly of the whale" experience!

One morning, while praying, I flipped open my Bible roulette style. The pages opened to Psalms. The first thing I saw was Psalms 41:1-2 *Blessed is he that considereth the* <u>*poor; the* LORD *will deliver him in time of trouble*</u>. *The* LORD *will preserve him and keep him alive; and he shall be blessed upon the earth; and thou wilt not deliver him unto the will of his enemies.* I do not remember reading that passage before. The words jumped off the page and into my troubled soul. I showed this revelation to my pastor and said, "God is going to make a way for me to pay that $1.5 million note."

I read and re-read that scripture. *Could God be telling me that He was able to deliver me out of this trouble?* Then, like a message from heaven, I suddenly remembered the pledge that I had made and paid, to help the poor many months before. Part of that money went to pay doctor bills for those who could not pay. Part went to clothe the needy in Africa. Part went to support missionaries. God had not forgotten about my kindness to others. God had not forgotten His guarantees ... His Word!

Within a few days after I read Psalms 41:1-2, I received a letter from the bank that stated, "The bank has canceled your $1.5 million note. You do not owe this bank one cent!" The other individuals were not released from the debt. Did I deserve that financial blessing? No. It was a gift from a loving God. I only obeyed His Word concerning giving to the poor; His Word protected my welfare.

The greatest financial insurance available is to go into partnership with God. He is the greatest business partner one could hope to have. He has a lot of opportunities in which to invest. Lost souls, feeding and clothing the needy, supporting missionaries and faith giving are just a few guaranteed investments that one can add to his or her portfolio. My faith is not in the FDIC or FSLIC, but in FIJC (Faith In Jesus Christ).

Let me show you the kind of insurance I am talking about. The Lord impressed me to give $30,000 on a special project to help the needy. This was completely out of character for me, but my wife and I felt very strongly about making the pledge. This was many months before we purchased the mall that foreclosed. In fact, I had forgotten about giving the money when my financial crisis arose, but God had not forgotten. No one told me, or asked me to give to this need; I just felt a strong impression to give, so I made the pledge. This pledge was to be paid over a period of one year. Those were my terms with the Lord, because I did not have the money at the time of the pledge. This is called faith giving. If I have the money in my pocket then it takes no faith to give it. But, when I do not have the money and I am impressed to pledge by faith, the Lord honors that commitment by providing the funds for the pledge.

Soon after my pledge, the stock market hit an all-time low. My stocks and bonds lost more than the amount that I had pledged. I told my wife that we were going to pay the pledge even if we had to sell our home to do so! Within a short time, God made a way for us to pay the pledge without selling anything. When my financial emergency arose, the Bank of Heaven and my advocate, Jesus Christ, responded quickly and resolved the problem in a way that I had never dreamed possible. Isn't that just like the Lord?

MAKING A PLEDGE—PAYING A PLEDGE

Never make a pledge unless you intend to pay it completely. One should make every effort to complete a commitment made to the work of the Lord at all cost. Breaking a vow to God is very serious and should be avoided. However, sometimes things change. There are some circumstances or conditions that may allow for reconsideration of a pledge. For example, a man and his wife made a pledge to a building program of their church. They were excited about the possibility of being able to help on the church expansion program. The sad part of this story is the fact that the man died before completely paying the pledge. Yet, the church board demanded that his widow pay the balance of the commitment. She was not financially able to pay and was ridiculed by her church. Just let common sense be the judge in this situation and one will conclude that the church was unethical in this case.

Another friend made a large pledge to their church for a building program. The church advertised in the big promotion production that the new facility would be started immediately. However, after many months no new construction had started. He asked about the delay and was told that the church board had decided to wait a few years to build. They said that they intended to place the pledged monies in a bank and collect interest until they decided to build. He said, "I want my money saving souls now, not collecting interest for some future venture that may never take place." I feel that he had just cause for rescinding his pledge. He appropriately placed his money in another program that would be productive for the Lord. He did not reduce the amount of money that he had pledged he just <u>re-directed it.</u>

A young couple was persuaded to sign the pledge card for the church. In fact they were told of the amount that they should pledge. Being God fearing young Christians and having absolute confidence in their pastor they agreed to the amount requested. This faithful couple has been making the pledge, but they are having problems paying their debts. The husband said, "We are striving to be cheerful givers, but to be honest with you, I have often given my pledge grudgingly." I can't believe that God is pleased with his children being debt-ridden just for the purpose of enlarging a sanctuary. I do not believe that God would judge this family harshly for canceling this pledge that resulted from man's peer pressure.

A pastor contacted me and said that the Lord had called him to start a mission church in Europe. He said, "I will be going there in just a few weeks." I was very excited about the opportunity to help in this mission effort. I promptly wrote him a check for $5,000. A year passed and the pastor had not gone anywhere. When I inquired about the delay he said, "I have had church problems in my home church and will not be able to leave for another year." I said, "I am sorry to hear that, but you told me that you were leaving immediately for Europe. Just send the money back and I will invest it in someone who does not have church problems." He said, "I don't have it, I spent the money on my home church." Needless to say I was very upset about the misuse of the funds I had given for European souls. This is just another example of how some folks will take advantage of your generosity.

When considering building programs it is good to review the methods that the Lord used in the past to provide for expansion. God gave Moses a very detailed plan for building a tent tabernacle and also commanded him to build it. How were the Israelites to meet the building costs? They were on their way out of slavery. They could not have had much to give. However, as we read on, we find the Israelites not only met the needs, but they were generous, so much so that they had to be told to stop giving! There was more than enough in the offering. *Then everyone came <u>whose heart was stirred, and everyone whose spirit was willing,</u> and they brought the LORD's offering for the work of the tabernacle of meeting, for all its service, and for the holy garments. They came, both men and women, as many as had a willing heart, and brought earrings and nose rings, rings and necklaces, all jewelry of gold, that is, every man who made an offering of gold to the LORD* (Exodus 35: 21-22, NSV). *The people bring much <u>more than enough</u> for the service of the work, which the LORD commanded to make. And Moses gave commandment, and they caused it to be proclaimed throughout the camp, saying, Let neither man nor woman make any more work for the offering of the sanctuary. So the people were restrained from bringing. For the stuff they had was sufficient for all the work to make it, and too much* (Exodus 36:5-7, *Amplified Bible*). When the Lord directs the expansion programs, they work!

I would like to make the following observations:

a. If the giving is truly for God's purpose, then His people will be willing to give even above the requirements.
b. If the giving is for God's purpose, the leaders will acknowledge when the requirements have been met and inform the people to stop giving.
c. Where did all these riches come from? When we

read Exodus 11:2-3 we will see that God planned the whole building project Himself and He did it perfectly. While the Israelites were still in Egypt, He told them to go to their Egyptian neighbors and ask for gold and silver. God gave them favor in the eyes of the Egyptians so that they received from the Egyptians enough gold for the Tabernacle. God had a plan for that gold, just as He has a plan for our finances.

Here is the point. **It was God's idea to build, so He gave the plan and He organized the funding. He also provided the source of funds from the people outside of His kingdom, who were unbelievers.** If we serve the same God we should have enough faith to let Him supply our needs for new buildings, or for anything else we need, for that matter.

I believe that God is just waiting for some of us to commit in our heart that we want to give as He directs. When God observes that we are following His leading, then He is free to abundantly bless us with finances, gained or earned, from our employment and/or business ventures.

GIVING TO THE NEEDY
Why was my $1.5 million debt cancelled when I only gave $30,000? The Dawsons gave $400,000 and were not blessed. We know that God is no respecter of persons and that He understands that $400,000 is much larger than $30,000. In fact I considered the other fellow to be a lot more spiritual than I. This was a mystery to me for a long time, until I searched God's Word for the answer. The friend in question sowed a lot more than I, but he did not reap a reward. As far as I know this benevolent brother gave cheerfully to a cause; yet, he was not blessed. Why? Was it that he did not invest in good ground? *Remember this: Whoever sows sparingly will also reap sparingly, and whoever sows*

generously will also reap generously. Each man should give what he has decided in his heart to give, not reluctantly or under compulsion, for God loves a cheerful giver. And God is able to make all grace abound to you, so that in all things at all times, having all that you need, you will abound in every good work. As it is written: He has scattered abroad his <u>gifts to the poor</u>; his righteousness endures forever. Now he who supplies seed to the sower and bread for food will also supply and increase your store of seed and will enlarge the harvest of your righteousness. <u>You will be made rich in every way</u> so that you can be generous on every occasion, and through us your generosity will result in thanksgiving to God. This service that you perform is not only supplying the needs of God's people but is also overflowing in many expressions of thanks to God. Because of the service by which you have proved yourselves, men will praise God for the obedience that accompanies your confession of the gospel of Christ, and for your generosity in <u>sharing with them and with everyone else</u> (II Corinthians 9:6-13, *NIV*).

The above verses solve the mystery. I gave to the poor as the Lord commands. My friend, as I stated before, gave according to the directive of a man. The financial seed he sowed went to advancing the lifestyle of his pastor. I was blessed because of the promise in the following verse. *You will be made rich in every way so that you can be generous on every occasion, and through us your generosity will result in thanksgiving to God* (2 Corinthians 9:11, *NIV*). This promise would work for the Dawsons as well, but they must obey God's Word as I did.

Did you know that there are many more commands and promises for God's people who give to the poor than any other form of giving in the Bible? As we read in the Bible, even a part of the tithe of the Old Testament was supposed to be set aside for the poor. (There will be more about tithes later.)

In Acts 10, the angel of the Lord arrested Cornelius' attention and aroused in him the reverential fear of the Lord. *"What is it, Lord?" he asked. The angel answered, "Your prayers and **gifts to the poor** have come up as a memorial offering before God"* (Acts 10:4, *NIV*). Not only were his prayers made a memorial before God, but our Savior also recorded his gifts to the poor! Giving to the poor seems to get God's attention. Have you started a memorial before God by giving to the poor?

A PREREQUISITE FOR SALVATION?
The following verses do not need an explanation.

- And the Lord said, *If there is a poor man among your brothers in any of the towns of the land that the LORD your God is giving you, do not be hardhearted or tightfisted toward your poor brother. Rather be openhanded and freely lend him whatever he needs ... Give generously to him and do so without a grudging heart; then because of this <u>the LORD your God will bless you in all your work and in everything you put your hand to</u>* (Deuteronomy 15:7-18, *NIV*).
- *A generous man will prosper; he who refreshes others <u>will himself be refreshed</u>* (Proverbs 11:25, *NIV*).
- *If your enemy is hungry, give him food to eat; if he is thirsty, give him water to drink. In doing this, you will heap burning coals on his head, and <u>the LORD will reward you</u>* (Proverbs 25:21-22, *NIV*).
- *What is pure religion? Religion that God our Father accepts as pure and faultless is this: <u>to look after orphans and widows in their distress</u> and to keep oneself from being polluted by the*

world (James 1:27, *NIV*).

- *He who gives to the poor will lack nothing, but he who closes his eyes to them receives many curses* (Proverbs 28:27, *NIV*).
- *Jesus answered, "If you want to be perfect, go, sell your possessions and give to the poor, and you will have treasure in heaven. Then come, follow me"* (Matthew 19:21, *NIV*).
- *... For I was hungry and you gave me something to eat, I was thirsty and you gave me something to drink, I was a stranger and you invited me in, I needed clothes and you clothed me, I was sick and you looked after me, I was in prison and you came to visit me. Then the righteous will answer him, `Lord, when did we see you hungry and feed you, or thirsty and give you something to drink? When did we see you a stranger and invite you in, or needing clothes and clothe you? When did we see you sick or in prison and go to visit you?' The King will reply, "I tell you the truth, whatever you did for one of the least of these brothers of mine, you did for me"* (Matthew 25:35-40, *NIV*).

Many times we hear the appeal, "Give to God, send your offerings to the Lord." Then we are advised to send the money to those making the appeal, as I pointed out earlier. Those who are asking us to support God are decked out in $3,000 suits, $1,000 shoes, Rolex watches and other items of prosperity. Matthew 25:40 gives us God's correct address. He indicates that He is with the poor and needy. And that is where we must send some of our offerings to the Lord.

In the following verse we find guaranteed salvation *...Come, you who are blessed by my Father; take your inheritance, the kingdom prepared for you since the creation of the world* (Matthew 25:34, *NIV*). What about those who do not care for the needy? *Then he will say to those on his left, "Depart from me, you who are cursed, into the eternal fire prepared for the devil and his angels. For I was hungry and you gave me nothing to eat, I was thirsty and you gave me nothing to drink, I was a stranger and you did not invite me in, I needed clothes and you did not clothe me, I was sick and in prison and you did not look after me." They also will answer, "Lord, when did we see you hungry or thirsty or a stranger or needing clothes or sick or in prison, and did not help you?" He will reply, "I tell you the truth, whatever you did not do for one of the least of these, you did not do for me." Then they will go away to eternal punishment, but the righteous to eternal life* (Matthew 25:41-46, *NIV*).

Can you be saved and neglect the poor and needy? Could verse 41-46 jeopardize your salvation? You might want to re-read Matthew 25:41-46 and prayerfully consider whether you conform, in order to ensure your salvation.

Please note that the Lord said, ... *I was hungry and you gave me nothing to eat* (Matthew 25:41). What if you gave funds to the church to feed the hungry and the church spent your offering on something else? Jesus makes it very clear that if you did not feed the hungry you would go into everlasting punishment. He did not say in verse 35 that you gave to the church, and the church gave me something to eat. Again he said YOU gave me something to eat. Hopefully, this will open your understanding on how important that you know and are ensured that your gifts are going to feed the hungry in this case. Many who collect for the needy, never feed the needy. It is your responsibility, as the giver, to make sure that you have obeyed Matthew 25: 31-46. Therefore, it is best to give directly to those who distribute the goods to the poor. Or better yet, to help distribute the goods and see first hand who is receiving your offering.

The Director of the American Red Cross was fired because she did not properly distribute 100% of the funds which had been collected for the victims of the World Trade Center disaster of 2001. The news media and others who had worked hard to raise money for these needy families were very upset that the Red Cross had directed those dedicated funds to other needs. We should insure that designated funds for the hungry actually attends to that need as the Lord directs.

HOW TO GIVE TO THE POOR

How should we give to the poor? *Be careful not to do your acts of righteousness before men, to be seen by them. If you do, you will have no reward from your Father in heaven. So when you give to the needy, do not announce it with trumpets, as the hypocrites do in the synagogues and on the streets, to be honored by men. I tell you the truth, they have received their reward in full. But when you give to the needy, do not let your left hand know what your right hand is doing, so that your giving may be in secret. Then your Father, who sees what is done in secret, will reward you* (Matthew 6:1-5, *NIV*).

Who is coming to dinner? *Then Jesus said to his host, "When you give a luncheon or dinner, do not invite your friends, your brothers or relatives, or your rich neighbors; if you do, they may invite you back and so you will be repaid. But when you give a banquet, invite the poor, the crippled, the lame, the blind, and you will be blessed. Although they cannot repay you, you will be repaid at the resurrection of the righteous"* (Luke 14:12-14, *NIV*).

DOES IT WORK?

I have included just a few examples in this book of how the Lord blessed me financially because I gave to the poor and needy. As I said earlier, if the Lord will bless me, He will bless you. God is no respecter of persons (Acts 10:34). The following are true-life stories of personal friends who took God at His Word, as I did, and gave to the underprivileged. The Lord blessed them as He had blessed others, and myself for obeying His Word.

ASK ALBERT

When I first met Al he was in a destitute condition. He was chemically dependent on many drugs. Also, he was separated from his wife with no chance of reconciliation. He said, "Ron, I need help, please help me." I told him that I could not help him, but that I could lead him to the One who could solve all his problems. I had the honor of leading Al through the plan of salvation and teaching him a series of Bible studies. His life completely changed in a short time.

Within a year, the Lord restored his previously deemed hopeless marriage. He then asked me how he should give to the Lord. By this time in my Christian life I was beginning to question some of the methods of giving as taught by some Christian groups. One thing that I did know for sure is that there are many scriptures in the Bible recommending us to help the needy. They all come with a guarantee for financial blessings. I related this to Al. He joined a program to help feed and clothe the hungry. Soon he was able to supply thousands of pounds of food and clothing to shelters around the nation. Al is now very wealthy. He does not pay tithes, but he supports the homeless, the widow, the aged and the orphaned. He has thanked me many times for sharing the truth that changed his and his family's lives for the better.

ASK MICHELLE

Another personal friend, who is a CPA, was having financial difficulties and relayed this information to me. This Christian lady had paid tithes all of her adult life, but for some reason she could not advance out of her financial rut. She knew that I had been blessed financially by giving to the Lord and wanted to know my secret. I told her the same thing that I told my friend Al.

About a year later she reminded me of the conversation

we had had about giving to the Lord. In fact, I had forgotten about our talk. She said, "When I started giving to the poor and other Christian activities, as you suggested, my income doubled in one year!" I said, "That is just like the Lord to honor His Word." This blessing occurred mid-2001.

This same friend wanted to take advantage of the zero percent financing incentives offered by car dealerships after the tragic terrorist events of September 11, 2001. She requested my assistance in locating a vehicle. Although I desperately needed to spend time with my property development business, I agreed to devote a whole Friday to help her get a car. We spent hours looking, test driving, and talking to car salesmen, but finally located a good deal on a new vehicle. While in route to the dealership we stopped to put the trade-in vehicle through a car wash. I saw a discarded Dallas newspaper on a table and flipped through until I located the classifieds. Out of curiosity, I scanned the automotive section and happened to find another vehicle listed at an unbelievable price. After the attendant finished cleaning the trade-in, we drove across the Metroplex to just check it out. Within two hours we reached an agreement; and by that same time the next day, my friend was the proud owner of a 1999 Mercedes ML320 at a price that was more than $10,000 below the actual value. While stunned with her new purchase, my friend tried to comprehend the blessings of God. She suddenly remembered a $2,000 dollar contribution made a month earlier to a church program that assists alcohol and drug addicts, the homeless, and the poor. God took her contribution and, less than two months later allowed it to multiply it into a $10,000 blessing. This is another example of how God's economy works; He takes our offering, looks at our heart and our needs, and provides accordingly. And yes, I was blessed as well when the very next day I sold a house that had been on the market for a long time.

ASK ANN

My mother-in-law, Ann, helped proof this study for me. She was shocked at some of the statements that I had written in this report. During the time she was reading this book one of her co-workers lost her home due to a fire. Her company employees were asked to raise money for this needy family. Ann said, "I hardly knew this lady; however, I gave her a large cash offering to help in her distress. More deliberately though, I gave to test what you had written in the book. To my surprise just a few days later, I received a large salary increase from my company." God will not lie! He will bless those who obey His commands that come with guarantees.

This is not a "name it, and claim it," "blab it and grab it" program that you might hear on the airwaves or other places. I am not saying that God will bless you if you give. I *am* saying that God will bless you for giving if you give according to the Scripture.

ASK GARY

Gary and his wife came to a Bible study that I was having in my home. They were new arrivals in town and had no knowledge of my writing this book. Someone at the Bible study asked me how my book on tithing was progressing. Gary and his wife jumped for joy when they learned of all the research I had completed to compile this manuscript. Then Gary told me the following account of how the Lord had dealt with him on giving. He said, "My wife and I tithed to our church for years, but we could never get ahead financially. We just lived from paycheck to paycheck. I knew that something was wrong with my giving but I did not know what the problem was. I had obeyed all my pastor had taught about tithing, but we went deeper and deeper into debt. My wife is a preachers daughter and was taught tithing all her life, but for some reason it seemed God was not pleased with our giving. Finally, in distress, I asked the Lord why he was not blessing us. His reply came loud and clear when He spoke to my heart, 'Your problem is paying tithes.' ".Wow! What a wake-up call that was. I then started an in-depth study on New Testament giving and found out that tithing is not part of the New Testament plan for Christians. And since I have started giving God's way we have been blessed." Gary told me of many books and Bible studies he had found on the subject of tithing. His conclusion was the same as the Apostle Paul, Peter and other New Testament giants; tithing is not for New Testament Christians.

WHO, AND WHEN SHOULD YOU HELP?

Just ask the Lord and He will show you who and when you should help. He said, *The poor will be with you always.* There are plenty of them around. The poor are not an endangered species. We will most likely run into them every day. In the next few sections of this chapter, I have included specific examples of giving which comply with the New Testament Scriptures.

The Widow (Single Mother)

While eating lunch recently, I asked the Lord whom I should give too. He said, "**That single mom waiting on your table, who is trying to provide for her children needs more than a 15 percent tip.**" Needless to say I left much more than the normal tip that day. It really is better to give than to receive. I would much rather be on the giving end, than to have to be on the receiving end. Think about it! If you give as God commands you will never need to be on the receiving end, except from Him!

The Missionary (Part of Five-Fold Ministry)

Just as the Lord directs you in other areas of your life, He will be quick to lead you to a financial need of others. The

Lord led me in the following manner to bless a missionary. We get excited about sending missionaries to the foreign field to tell the lost world about Jesus. Partners in Missions and other worthy monetary programs support these dedicated souls for their journey into the faraway places of ministry. But, what about their support when they return home after their assignment is completed? Many missionaries who have been away from home for many months or years most likely will have very few possessions or property when they come home.

One such missionary family returned from Russia after a long period of labor for Jesus in that country. They had nothing to come home to but an old run-down car that was a disgrace, to say the least. In fact, their two small children were so embarrassed that they would lay down in the back seat when their missionary parents drove the old car down the street.

They stopped in my city to visit friends and family a few days after their return from Russia. My family was excited to learn about all of the many miracles and salvations that they experienced while on the mission field. I knew them from my college days. We were not members of the same Christian organization, but I was aware of their sacrifices for the lost.

I had a very nice Lincoln Towncar for sale when they came by. It was almost new. The price was right. But for some reason it would not sell. A few days after their visit the strangest impression came to me to give the missionaries a good deal on the Lincoln. "That was a foolish thought. They do not have enough money to put gas in the car," I said to myself. A few days passed and the more I looked at that car, the less I liked seeing it on my property. Then for some strange reason I was afraid to drive it fearing I would damage the car and for sure could not sell it. I was tormented for days when I considered the fact that I had too many cars, while that precious missionary couple only had one old, decrepit car. Finally, I called the missionary and told him to come and get this Lincoln off my property. I said, "You can make $100 a month payments or whatever you can spare." After just a few payments I sent him the title free and clear and told him that the car was a gift for his labor for the Lord. He was blessed, and his kids could sit high while passing through town. But most of all I was blessed. When I gave him the car it was like a 500-pound weight had been removed from my soul. I found the true meaning that it is more blessed to give than to receive. And yes, the Lord paid me back for that Lincoln many times over since my act of generosity.

The Aliens

We have all been bombarded by the beggars on the street corners holding up their sign saying, "I will work for food." Of course most of those folks have no intention of working and just want a handout. But there is another group that I pass every Sunday morning on my way to church who wants to work and will work for an honest days pay. These poor Hispanic men are trying to get a few bucks just to feed their families.

A few Sundays ago my wife and I passed such a group standing on the streets wanting someone to hire them for the day. Of course there is not much need for workers on Sunday morning. As we drove by these 10 unemployed men, the following Bible verse awoke in my spirit; *It is more blessed to give than to receive* (Acts 20:35, *NIV*). I have always said that I had rather be on the giving end than have to be on the receiving end of the equation. I was reminded of the following familiar passage by Jesus that states, *Freely you have received, freely give* (Matthew 10:8, *NIV*).

That new, crisp $100 bill, that I had hid in the secret place of my wallet seemed to say, "Let me out of here, those men need help." The further I drove away from that scene the more pressure I felt to go back and help them in some way. I finally told my wife that I was going to stop at the little store ahead and change that $100 bill to 10 $10 bills and give it to those men on the street. We both got excited about this gift. I drove back to the workers, stopped my car, rolled my window down, and here they came running for work. I handed each one a $10 bill and said, "God bless you" and drove off. I am sure that they thought I was out of my mind. But I can tell you my wife and I felt like we floated to the church after that. We found Jesus' address that day.

The Orphans

A few years ago I had the opportunity to support six children in an orphanage in India. These kids were living in very destitute conditions with no chance for their life to improve. When I learned that it only would take $100 per month to provide adequate food, clothing, shelter, and education for the children, I eagerly committed to support this need. I knew that the money was going directly to Jesus as He commanded in the 25th chapter of Matthew.

The Sick

In order to be obedient to the Scriptures regarding visiting the sick, I was unsure of how to proceed. It doesn't take a genius to come to the logical conclusion that the sick can be found in our hospitals! Thus I proceeded directly to the closest hospital with a stack of signed get-well cards and small New Testament Bibles under my arm. I walked the corridors of the hospital looking for patients who had no visitors. These lonely people were eager to see a friendly face and were very receptive to my visit. The card and Bible were readily accepted. I received an immediate blessing just watching their faces light up from having a visitor who cared. I challenge you to follow my example and experience the thrill of being the hands and feet of Jesus.

A friend's teenage daughter was in a terrible automobile accident. They had no insurance and the medical bills were projected to exceed $10,000. My wife and I prayed about this catastrophe. We asked ourselves this question, "If this was our daughter and we had no way to provide medical attention, would we want help?" Of course the answer was yes. We paid the medical expenses through the church and the family involved never knew the source of the blessing. The Lord knew all about our gift. He said in the New Testament that if you give in secret He would reward in public.

The Prisoners

This is one command that some have a hard time obeying because of the difficulty involved in trying to visit a prison. But, there are other ways to help the prisoner. For example, I have a good friend who was sentenced to 41 years in a Federal Prison. It is almost impossible to visit him because of all the regulations required to enter the penitentiary. However, his family has many financial needs. He had rather me send money to his wife and two small children than visit him. My wife and I have helped this family for a long time. In fact we have helped on his attorney fees because we believe, as do many others, that he is innocent. Jesus did not qualify the prisoner you are to visit as to whether he is guilty or innocent. He just said visit them.

BEWARE OF THE ENEMY

I feel I would be remiss if I did not address one other issue at this point. There has been so much prosperity preaching and faith preaching in the last 30-40 years that some people have mistakenly gotten the idea that living by faith and giving by faith means they will have no more problems or struggles in life. I do not believe that is the intended message. So, with regard to this message, it is imperative to understand that obeying God's giving plan does not prevent lawsuits, losses on business deals, or loss of personal property and/or income. The devil will still attack, but the bottom line is always what counts in any business deal. No matter what the devil tries to destroy, the Lord will more than replace it if you have obeyed His commands. I have come to the place mentally where I consider an attack by the enemy to be a blessing in the making.

For example, a few years ago I gave $1,500 to a special need of which I had been made aware. This was a worthy hardship and I felt like the Lord was leading me to give. On my way home that night it started raining very hard. As I entered the house I could hear and see water coming through the roof and down onto the floor. The first thought that popped into my mind was, *You are so foolish, your giving was not directed by the Lord. You just wanted attention. You should have kept that money and fixed the roof.* Of course, we know where thoughts like that originate. The next day the roof repairman gave me an estimate. You guessed it, $1,500. The thoughts of how foolish I was came back again. A couple of days later we experienced a major hailstorm in our area. The hail really did a job on my roof. This situation was covered by my homeowner's insurance. Not only did we get a new roof, but we also had several thousand dollars left over after the job was completed. I was quick to remind the evil spirit about my giving and receiving.

Look what happened to Job. The devils' attack on Job made him twice as wealthy at the bottom line. So, do not make the mistake of believing that your giving God's way will make you immune to trouble or hardship. It will not. What it will do, however, is give you the guarantees of blessing that go along with obedience to the commands.

As we have seen from these scriptures and from the testimonies, when giving is done by God's directive, then His Word ensures certain blessings for the giver. If we truly want to be blessed we must give according to God's Word. Giving because of the word of a man offers no insurance of blessing for the giver. God's commands are the only insurance we have that our actions will provide blessing.

Part II

CHAPTER FIVE

The Story of the Tithe – Before the Law

In this chapter we will begin our look at the history of giving and tithing which existed before the Law.

The Hebrew word translated "tithe" is *masêr,* which simply means "a tenth part." Tithe is not a religious expression, but a mathematical expression. The Greek counterpart to this word is *d kate,* meaning "the tenth." Giving, according to the New Testament, should not be a requirement based on arithmetic, but based on an attitude of the heart as stated in 2 Corinthians 9:6-7:

> *But this I say: "He who sows sparingly will also reap sparingly, and he who sows bountifully will also reap bountifully. So let each one give as he purposes in his heart, not grudgingly or of necessity; for God loves a cheerful giver"* (NKJV).

Given this, let us ask the questions: Is tithing a New Testament command? What is our responsibility, and how should we give to the Lord? For the answers, let us first look in the Old Testament at the tithing and/or offerings given by seven biblical characters that lived prior to the Law. Please prayerfully consider the following.

Cain and Abel

In Genesis 4 we find the first offerings to God recorded in the Bible; these were the offerings of Cain and Abel. Again, we see these offerings were voluntary. There is no command recorded in the Bible to give them. **We do read that the Lord was pleased with Abel's offering and displeased with Cain's offering.** The biblical record does not indicate that either of them offered a tenth. We do see that Abel's offering was acceptable to God while Cain's was not. Therefore we need to understand what God considers acceptable. This is a good example of how one can give an unpleasing gift, if it is not given in accordance with divine instructions!

By faith Abel offered God a better sacrifice than Cain did. By faith he was commended as a righteous man, when God spoke well of his offerings. And by faith he still speaks, even though he is dead (Hebrews 11:4, *NIV*).

Noah

Another occurrence of giving recorded in Genesis was that of Noah in Chapter 8. Please note that there was no command for a tenth to be offered. Actually, there was no command to give at all. Noah gave because he loved the Lord. The Scripture says he gave *some* (not a tenth) of what he had; as we see in the following scripture: *Then Noah built an altar to the LORD and, taking some of all the clean animals and clean birds, he sacrificed burnt offerings on it* (Genesis 8:20).

Job

According to Hubert Krause and Orest Solyma, *History of tithing from the Bible,* "There is no reference to tithing when

Job's vast wealth is discussed. He is described by God as blameless and righteous, fearing God and shunning evil. Job describes himself as:

- Giving to the needy and to the poor (Job 29:12-16; 30:25; 31:16-19)
- Taking care of the widow (Job 31:16)
- Taking care of the orphan (Job 31:17-18)

How is it that, in reminding God of his good deeds, Job never once, as part of his defense, mentions any 'faithfulness in tithing?' To whom would he have tithed?" This is a very good example of a righteous man for whom we have no recording of tithing.

Abram

The first record of tithing, or giving a tenth, is described in Genesis 14:20 when Abram, whose name was later changed to Abraham, tithed to Melchizedek. This is referred to in the New Testament.

For this Melchizedek, king of Salem, priest of the Most High God, who met Abraham returning from the slaughter of the kings and blessed him; to whom also Abraham gave a tenth part of all; first being interpretation King of righteousness, and after that also King of Salem, which is King of peace; (Hebrews 7:1-2).

Please note that this tithe, or tenth, was not a required amount, but an amount that was given from the heart. This was before the Law that established tithing some 430 years later. The important thing to see here is that in Genesis the word "tithe" did not refer to a required offering, but a voluntary offering. The tithe of Abraham, and later Jacob, was a freewill gifts and was not, strictly speaking, the same as tithes given under the Mosaic Law. There is no indication that Melchizedek either demanded or requested a tenth. Abram gave a tithe in reverence to God for what the Lord had done for him, not because it was required of him. After returning from rescuing Lot and defeating his enemies, Abraham met Melchizedek, the King of Salem and priest of the Most High God. The text simply states that Abraham gave Melchizedek a tithe of all the goods he had <u>obtained in battle.</u>

There is no recorded demand of Abraham for a tenth. In fact, there is no other record of Abram giving another tenth to Melchizedek during his entire life span. Neither is there an explanation given why Abraham gave a tithe to Melchizedek.

Did Abram give a tenth of all he owned, or a tenth of what he had taken in battle? Hebrews 7:4 records that he gave a tenth of the spoils. This means he gave only a tenth of what he had taken from others. He had taken treasures from five kings in battle, so his spoils could have been very large. The point here is that he gave freely. He was not required to pay a tithe. He gave out of his heart to the man of God.

Is this one act of freely giving a tenth an adequate reference for demanding tithes from New Testament Christians today? Is tithing part of Christian economics? Let us examine the custom as to why Abram gave this tenth to Melchizedek. In about 1900 B.C., when the kings Amraphel, Arioch, Kedorlaomer and Tidal captured Sodom and Gomorrah, they claimed Abram's nephew Lot and his possessions. Abram took 318 of his men and routed Kedorlaomer and his allies and recaptured all the goods that were taken, including Lot and his possessions. Melchizedek, Priest of the Most High God, then blessed Abram. He acknowledged that God had delivered Abram's enemies into his hands.

It was customary in ancient times, and was well established, that landlords could claim or were entitled to a ten percent fee (tenth of the crops) from those who used the land to make a living. Further, it was a common practice in Abram's day to pay the "Kings Tenth" as illustrated in I Samuel 8:14-17. *He will take the best of your fields and vineyards and olive groves and give them to his attendants. He will take a tenth of your grain and of your vintage and give it to his officials and attendants. Your menservants and maidservants and the best of your cattle and donkeys he will take for his own use. He will take a tenth of your flocks, and you yourselves will become his slaves (NIV).*

Giving a tenth of anything to the king was not the same as giving a tithe to the Lord. Furthermore, the king's tenth was not holy, whereas the tithe given to the Lord was holy. Abram recognized that God was the true owner of the spoils since He made the victory possible. Abram proceeded to give Melchizedek a tenth of the spoils to remind himself that God was High Priest and rightful owner, and was, therefore, entitled to a portion of the spoils as a result of the victory (See Genesis 14:17-20).

The Lord then promised Abram, as recorded in Genesis 15:18-20, that his descendants would be given the land. The Lord's covenant was established and Abraham's belief was credited as righteousness. The promise was not only to Abram, but to his descendants as well.

As mentioned in Chapter 3, Psalms 112 states another promise to *all* those who obey the commands of God *Blessed is the man who fears the LORD ... His children will be mighty in the land; the generation of the upright will be blessed. Wealth and riches are in his house ... He will have no fear of bad news; his heart is steadfast, trusting in the LORD. His heart is secure, he will have no fear; in the end he will look in triumph on his foes. He has scattered abroad his gifts to the poor* (Psalms 112, *NIV*). This is not part of the Law; this is another of God's promises, or guarantees. God's guarantees are as trustworthy as the biblical doctrines of the virgin birth, the resurrection, and the second coming of Jesus! We can count on God to make good on His promises.

In review, we see that Abram, victorious over the armies of the kings, had rescued his nephew Lot and brought back all the goods and captives previously taken by enemies. He was met by Melchizedek, priest of the Most High God, who blessed him and to whom Abram gave *tithes of all* or, as most translations render it, *a tenth of everything.* The Bible does not say that Abram was obeying a law that *required* him to give a tenth.

Jacob

Jacob, the grandson of Abraham, who lived long before the Law of Moses was given, promised that he would give the Lord a tenth of all he received. We read in Genesis 28 that Jacob promised the Lord a tenth <u>if He would bless him.</u> *Then Jacob made a vow, saying, "If God will be with me and will watch over me on this journey I am taking and will give me food to eat and clothes to wear so that I return safely to my father's house, then the LORD will be my God and this stone that I have set up as a pillar will be God's house, and of all that you give me I will give you a tenth"* (Genesis 28:20-22, *NIV*). This was not a request from God but more of an act of faith from Jacob to the Lord, a commitment with a promise to pay if he is blessed. It is not a law from God. Jacob was really saying, "God, if you give me safety and blessings then I will give you a tenth."

Was this a command from the Lord or a personal vow? God did not need to go into business with Jacob in order to earn a mere 10% on the deal. God owned everything and Jacob understood that. He negotiated with God for help. Read the verse again and note that he said, *If you will be with me ... watch over me ... give me food ... and clothes ... so that I return safely to my father house ... I will give you a tenth.* Jacob made this vow when he was camped at Bethel.

While fleeing from his brother Esau, he had a dream in which the Lord confirmed His covenant with Abraham and his descendants. After he awoke, he became afraid because he believed that he was in the Lord's House, the Gate to Heaven. The next morning, Jacob asked for God's protection and aid. He told God that he would give Him a tenth of everything. Again, this tradition of giving ten percent had its roots in the ancient landlord/tenant/king relationship.

The Lord honored Jacob's prayer. As we all know, he became the father of the twelve tribes that would become the nation of Israel. This man of faith had enough audacity to challenge God for help. God took him up on that challenge and blessed him. Do you have enough faith to test God for a blessing? He loves such loyal faith. God wants us to Test Him, Trust Him, and Try Him to see if He will not bless us.

In light of understanding the cultural and social expectations in which Abraham and Jacob lived, it can easily be rationalized that the tenth given by Abram and Jacob was not equivalent to the tithe as set forth by the Law of Moses. The tenth of the spoils paid by Abram was for his victory and Jacob's tenth was for God to watch over him and for a safe journey. There is no evidence in the Bible to indicate that Abram or Jacob intended to give an annual on-going tenth of their future gains. Why would they? The Levites, priesthood and the tabernacle would not exist for another 430 years following Abram's victory. Abram was only trying to give his due to God, who is the ultimate landowner, Eternal King, and High Priest (Most High God) who makes victory possible.

<u>Joseph</u>

Hubert Krause and Orest Solyma, *History of tithing from the Bible*, states, "As ruler of Egypt, Joseph decreed that the Egyptians, who owned land acquired from Pharaoh to pay the king one-fifth (20%) of their crops for the 7-year period of good seasons. If he had been aware of a universal tithing law one would assume that, as a principle, one-tenth, rather that one-fifth, of the crops would have been demanded.

The patriarchs were spiritual leaders in their own right, so to whom would these patriarchs have regularly tithed? There is abundant evidence of offerings and sacrifices. However, regular tithing cannot be accounted for adequately. Patriarchal sacrifices, offerings, and voluntary gifts are expressions from the heart and are personal expressions of divine blessings. It is clear that the patriarchs expressed gratitude, generosity and worship, and associated these with the concept of first fruits, firstlings and offerings."

God did not institute tithing in Genesis, not in Genesis 4 (Cain and Abel), in Genesis 8 (Noah), in Genesis 12 or 14 (Abraham), nor in Genesis 28 (Jacob). There was no statement from God regarding tithing in either case. There is no continuous law of tithing recorded anywhere in the Scriptures. There is no case for tithing as a pre-Law obligation to God. Would the Lord demand something without revealing to men exactly what He required? Genesis gives no record of God demanding a tenth, although there was required giving to ruling kings before the Mosaic Law. We read, *Let Pharaoh do this, and let him appoint officers over the land, and take up the fifth part of the land of Egypt in the seven plenteous years* (Genesis 41:34). This 20% giving was only required for seven years in order to have abundant food supplies during the famine.

In review, by studying these biblical characters that lived *before* the Law, we can conclude that tithing was not *required* before the Law. Tithing was a freewill gift, often a one-time event, which was given to honor the Lord with one's wealth. Abraham's tithe to Melchizedek is probably the most used scripture to teach that Christians should tithe today. However, we just learned that this one-time act of generosity was a voluntary gift from the heart, and was not a requirement. Is this enough evidence to convince you to believe that God *requires* you, as a New Testament believer, to tithe or face the consequences if you do not? It is not nearly enough evidence to convince me.

We will read in the next chapter about the established Law of Tithing as commanded in the Old Testament.

CHAPTER SIX

The Law

Throughout history, God related to His people differently according to the dispensation in which they lived. These dispensations can be loosely grouped into the pre-Law era, the period of the Law, and the dispensation of grace (the New Testament Church). We cannot get a clear picture of the truth regarding any biblical subject, including tithing, until we understand how God dealt with His people on that subject in each of these dispensations. In the previous chapter we looked at tithing before the Law. In this chapter, we will look at tithing from the standpoint of the Law. This progression is necessary if we are going to see the correct application in the New Testament.

Under the Law, ten percent of agricultural and animal production was set aside each year. The intent behind the sacrifices, offerings, and tithing law was so that the whole Israelite society should benefit. First and foremost, it was for the purpose of keeping God's feasts.

Leviticus 27:30-33 stated that the tithe of the land would include the seed of the land and the fruit of the tree. In addition, the Hebrew people were required to set apart every tenth animal of their herds and flocks. This is called the Lord's tithe or the Levites' tithe. This tithe was to be divided among the Levites. *A tithe of everything from the land, whether grain from the soil or fruit from the trees, belongs to the LORD; it is holy to the LORD. If a man redeems any of his tithes, he must add a fifth of the value to it. The entire tithe of the herd and flock—every tenth animal that passes under the shepherd's rod—will be holy to the LORD. He must not pick out the good from the bad or make any substitution. If he does make a substitution, both the animal and its substitute become holy and cannot be redeemed* (Leviticus 27:30-33, *NIV*).

The Law of Moses presents the purpose of the tithe as three-fold. First, it was reparation to the Levites for their lack of an inheritance of land that the other eleven tribes received. Second, it was payment to the priests who were responsible to teach the Torah to all of Israel. Third, it was to care for the poor, orphan, and widow. After the Exodus, the Lord instructed Moses to single out the tribe of Levi and to appoint them to be in charge of the Tabernacle. They were not to be included in the census or counted with the other tribes of Israel. They were to be set apart. *The LORD had said to Moses: "You must not count the tribe of Levi or include them in the census of the other Israelites. Instead, appoint the Levites to be in charge of the tabernacle of the Testimony— over all its furnishings and everything belonging to it. They are to carry the tabernacle and all its furnishings; they are to take care of it and encamp around it. Whenever the tabernacle is to move, the Levites are to take it down, and whenever the tabernacle is to be set up, the Levites shall do it. Anyone else who goes near it shall be put to death* (Numbers 1:47-51, *NIV*).

The Lord further states that the Levites would have no inheritance of land but would be given the tithe instead (Numbers 18:20-32). To summarize, the purpose of the biblical tithe was: (1) to care for the Levites who were denied land, (2) to provide subsistence for the priesthood whose function was to preach the Torah, and (3) to care for the poor in general.

The Levites were one of the twelve tribes of Israel; they were priests and Temple assistants. The tithe, or tenth, was a taxation on the other eleven tribes <u>to supply the needs of Levites</u>. Numbers 18:21-32 stated that the tithes would be given to the Levites, because the Levites did not receive a land inheritance like the other tribes. The Levites' duty was to offer a Heave Offering to the Lord. This would constitute a tithe on the part of the goods which they received. The rest of the goods which the Levites received would provide their living as the reward for their work in the Tabernacle.

TITHE OF THE TITHES

Tithe of the tithes—The tithes of all the produce of the fields were brought to the Levites. **Out of these a tenth part was given to the priests**. This is called the tithe of the tithes. This Law is found in Numbers 18:21-32.

*I give to the Levites all the tithes in Israel as their inheritance in return for the work they do while serving at the Tent of Meeting ... They will receive no inheritance among the Israelites. Instead, I give to the Levites as their inheritance the tithes that the Israelites present as an offering to the LORD ... The LORD said to Moses, "Speak to the Levites and say to them: 'When you receive from the Israelites the tithe I give you as your inheritance, <u>you must pre-sent **a tenth of that tithe** as the Lord's offering</u>. Your offering will be reckoned to you as grain from the threshing floor or juice from the winepress ... from these tithes you must give the Lord's portion to Aaron the priest. You must present as the Lord's portion the best and holiest part of everything given to you.' ... for it is your wages for your work* *at the Tent of Meeting"* (Numbers 18:21-32, *NIV*).

The Levites *were to **tithe on the tithe** they received and this tithe went to the priest.* In other words, the priest received 10%, not 100% of the tithe, as taught by some groups today.

*As it is also written in the Law, we will bring the firstborn of our sons and of our cattle, of our herds and of our flocks to the house of our God, to the priests ministering there. Moreover, we will bring to the storerooms of the house of our God, to the priests, the first of our ground meal, of our grain offerings, of the fruit of all our trees and of our new wine and oil. And we will bring a tithe of our crops to the Levites, for it is the Levites who collect the tithes in all the towns where we work. A priest descended from Aaron is to accompany the Levites when they receive the tithes, and the Levites are to bring a **tenth of the tithes** up to the house of our God, to the storerooms of the treasury. The people of Israel, including the Levites, are to bring their contributions of grain, new wine and oil to the storerooms where the articles for the sanctuary are kept and where the ministering priests, the gatekeepers and the singers stay. We will not neglect the house of our God* (Nehemiah 10:36-39, *NIV*).

Again we see the priest received a tenth of the tithe for their wages. The priest was only one division of the Levites. It appears that the other 90% was designated for other ministries and the needy. The Levites performed numerous duties within the nation of Israel. Following are some of their occupations:

- Teachers (Deuteronomy 24:8; 33:10; 2 Chronicles 35:3)
- Judges (Deut 17:8-9; 21:5; 1 Chronicles 23:4)
- Medical Services (Leviticus 13:2; 14:2; Luke 17:14)

- Singers (1 Chronicles 25:1-31; 2 Chronicles 5:12; 34:12)
- Writers (1 Chronicles 2:55; 2 Chronicles 34:13)
- Architects (2 Chronicles 34:8-13)

THE LEVITE, THE ALIEN, THE FATHERLESS, AND THE WIDOW

Other purposes for the Old Testament tithe are listed in the following Scriptures.

*When you have finished setting aside a tenth of all your produce in the **third year**, the year of the tithe, you shall give it to the **Levite, the alien, the fatherless and the widow,** so that they may eat in your towns and be satisfied. Then say to the LORD your God: "I have removed from my house the sacred portion and have given it to the Levite, the alien, the fatherless and the widow, according to all you commanded. I have not turned aside from your commands nor have I forgotten any of them. I have not eaten any of the sacred portion while I was in mourning, nor have I removed any of it while I was unclean, nor have I offered any of it to the dead. I have obeyed the LORD my God; I have done everything you commanded me. Look down from heaven, your holy dwelling place, and bless your people Israel and the land you have given us as you promised on oath to our forefathers, a land flowing with milk and honey"* (Deuteronomy 26:12-15, *NIV*).

Additional scriptures dealing with the tithe are as follows: Deuteronomy 12:5-7, 11-12, 17-19, and 14:24-29. What the Lord commanded the people to do with their tithe and offerings in these scriptures (which are discussed below) is a surprising revelation to many. It shouldn't be. If, when tithing is taught in the New Testament church, why isn't it taught thoroughly? And why is it not adhered to thoroughly by those in the ministry? The average Christian knows very little about the Old Testament tithe, and when it comes to applying it to himself, all he knows is that he "owes" God 10% of his income. If he does not pay it, he is robbing God, or so he is taught. If this has been your understanding, you will most likely be surprised when you read the next few verses.

HAVE YOU PAID YOURSELF A TITHE?

But you are to seek the place the LORD your God will choose from among all your tribes to put his Name there for his dwelling. To that place you must go; there bring your burnt offerings and sacrifices, your tithes and special gifts, what you have vowed to give and your freewill offerings, and the firstborn of your herds and flocks. There, in the presence of the LORD your God, you and your families shall eat and shall rejoice in everything you have put your hand to, because the LORD your God has blessed you (Deuteronomy 12:5-7, *NIV*).

You must not eat in your own towns the tithe of your grain and new wine and oil, or the firstborn of your herds and flocks, or whatever you have vowed to give, or your freewill offerings or special gifts. Instead, you are to eat them in the presence of the LORD your God at the place the LORD your God will choose—you, your sons and daughters, your menservants and maidservants, and the Levites from your towns—and you are to rejoice before the LORD your God in everything you put your hand to.

*Be careful not to neglect the Levites as long as you
live in your land* (Deuteronomy 12:17-19, *NIV*).

*But if that place is too distant and you have been
blessed by the L*ORD *your God and cannot carry
your tithe (because the place where the L*ORD *will
choose to put his Name is so far away), then
exchange your tithe for silver, and take the silver
with you and go to the place the L*ORD *your God
will choose. Use the silver to buy whatever you
like: cattle, sheep, wine or other fermented drink,
or anything you wish. Then you and your household shall eat there in the presence of the L*ORD
*your God and rejoice. And do not neglect the
Levites living in your towns, for they have no
allotment or inheritance of their own. At the end
of every three years, bring all the tithes of that
year's produce and store it in your towns, so that
the Levites (who have no allotment or inheritance
of their own) and the aliens, the fatherless and
the widows who live in your towns may come and
eat and be satisfied, and so that the L*ORD *your
God may bless you in all the work of your hands*
(Deuteronomy 14:24-29, *NIV*).

These verses show that the people, not the Levites, were
commanded to take their tithes to the place the Lord prescribed (or the city of Jerusalem) and have a party! They
could sell their tithe, or exchange their tithe for whatever they
wanted. They could buy cattle, wine, or other fermented
drink, or anything they wanted. The *King James Version* says
strong drink. It's in the book. Read it for yourself.

I had to review the scriptures again and again to see how
the tithes and offerings were to be utilized. I am sure you
will have to do likewise. These passages positively instruct

the people to spend the tithe and offering on themselves and their families. How often do you hear this in New Testament churches? There was no command for them to give the entire tithe to anyone. They were only requested to remember the Levites, the aliens, the fatherless and the widow. Also, note that this was to be accomplished only every third year. Again, how often do we hear this in New Testament churches? We do not. Instead we hear year after year that if we do not tithe we are robbing the Lord.

ALLOCATION OF TITHES

In the Old Testament the purpose of giving a tenth was to meet the material need of **the Levite, the stranger, the fatherless (the orphan), and the widow.** *When you have finished laying aside all the tithe of your increase in the third year—the year of tithing—and have given it to the **Levite, the stranger, the fatherless, and the widow,** so that they may eat within your gates and be filled, then you shall say before the LORD your God: "I have removed the holy tithe from my house, and also have given them to the **Levite, the stranger, the fatherless, and the widow,** according to all Your commandments which You have commanded me; I have not transgressed Your commandments, nor have I forgotten them"* (Deuteronomy 26:12-13, NIV).

Please note that the tithe is to go to the Levite, the stranger, the fatherless and the widow according to God's Word. How should the tithe be divided among the Levite, the stranger, the fatherless and the widow? What percent should each group receive? Are modern Christian organizations distributing the tithe to **the stranger? The widow? The fatherless?** In the New Testament the ministers are considered by most to be modern day Levites. So, should the five-fold ministry listed in Ephesians 4:11 as apostles, prophets, evangelists, pastors and teachers be paid equally? What about missionaries? By what celestial authority do some receive more than others?

The tithe was an expression of gratitude to God by His people. Basic to tithing was the acknowledgment of God's ownership of everything. As Nehemiah records, *I also realized that the portions for the Levites had not been given them; for each of the Levites and the singers who did the work had gone back to his field. So I contended with the rulers, and said, "Why is the house of God forsaken?" And I gathered them together and set them in their place. Then all Judah brought the tithe of the grain and the new wine and the oil to the storehouse. And I appointed as treasurers over the storehouse Shelemiah the priest and Zadok the scribe, and of the Levites, Pedaiah; and next to them was Hanan the son of Zaccur, the son of Mattaniah; for they were considered faithful, and their task **was to distribute to their brethren*** (Nehemiah 13:10-12, *NIV*). This was their system of distribution.

Was the tithe for the priest only? It appears there were several divisions of the Levites who were in charge of the work of the Lord. As indicated above, there was a distribution system of the tithes from the storehouse to each of the workers. May I ask those who believe New Testament Christians should tithe, how and who decides the distribution of the so-called tithes? The poor missionaries must crisscross the country begging for years just to raise adequate support. The Sunday school teachers are not paid, yet they work many hours studying and preparing. This is often in addition to all their family and vocational responsibilities. Many young ministers are living below the poverty level while they put in as many hours, or more than the senior ministers. Is that what the Lord intended? I do not believe so.

UNDERSTANDING BIBLICAL TITHING

How well do we, as Christians, really understand the principle of biblical tithing in relation to its origins, purpose, and applications? We must ask ourselves if tithing is biblically mandated for the church, as many church pastors claim, to avoid stealing from God (Malachi 3:8-12). Or, is tithing part of the Old Testament Law of Moses similar to circumcision, temple sacrifices, offerings, etc? What was its purpose?

The true biblical tithe commanded of Israel was performed on a seven-year cycle called the Shemittah Cycle.

The tithe actually consisted of fruit, grain, wine and later; animals, that are typically harvested as agriculture products from the land. It never consisted of money. Further, the Lord commanded and the Law of Moses recorded that a tithe of everything from the land belonged to the Lord (Levites 27:30-33).

Throughout the Bible we find the use of a monetary system in force for most of the ages. There was a monetary society as well as bartering systems. This is an important consideration because everyone did not have occupations related to agriculture. Agriculture products were the only items that were to be received as tithes. Money was never used to pay tithes in the Bible. The Law of Tithing only affected the farmers.

During the Festival Tithe (ma'aser sheni), money or silver used as currency in ancient times was not an allowable substitution for the tithe. Tithes were collected annually and were based upon one's product increase for the year. The Israelis gathered their tithes together and took them to the "presence of the Lord" at the pre-determined location of His House.

As discussed in previous chapters, it was also expected that the needs of the Levites would be met on an annual basis by the first tithe or the Levitical Tithe (ma'aser rishon; see Deuteronomy 14:27, 12:19). Also, **every third year**, the Israelite was required to store his tithe in his own town to **feed the fatherless, aliens, and widows**. This was the tithe of the poor (ma'aser ani; see Deuteronomy 14:22-29, 26:12-15 and Amos 4:4-5).

REVIEW OF OLD TESTAMENT TITHING

In review: Biblical tithing was based on one's produce (products from the land) increase for the year. This was accomplished annually on a **seven-year cycle** called the Shemittah Cycle. This tithe had to be eaten in the presence of the Lord and was collected on the 1st, 2nd, 4th, and 5th years only. The third tithe was the **tithe of the poor** to be collected on the 3rd and 6th years only. **No tithe was collected on the 7th year or Sabbatical year.** The farmers were to let the land rest in that year.

Please note that the 3rd and 6th year the tithe went to the poor, strangers, fatherless and widows (Deuteronomy 26-12-13). There was no tithe in the 7th year. Therefore, out of a seven-year cycle the Levites only received the tithes on the 1st, 2nd, 4th, and 5th year. Do churches that preach tithing only collect tithes four out of seven years? I dare say that you have never heard that preached!

It is also interesting to note that the seventh year, the Lord commanded a Sabbath rest for the land. *But in the seventh year the land is to have a Sabbath rest, a Sabbath to the Lord ... whatever the land yields during the Sabbath year will be food for you—for yourself, your man servants and maid servants, and the hired workers and temporary resident who live among you ...* (Leviticus 25:4-7, *NIV*). There is no command for tithing from that yield that grew of itself without cultivation.

To refute those who would claim that tithes had to be agricultural products because there was no monetary system in place at that time, I offer the following examples of economic systems in use during the Old Testament period. The Bible reveals that the tithe was never money; it was always produce from the land. Money in the form of precious metals (usually silver) in the time of Abraham and coinage in Roman times was frequently used in ancient societies. Abraham purchased a field with silver measured in shekels

(100 shekels) to bury his wife Sarah in Genesis 23:15-16. Jacob purchased land with pieces of silver as recorded in Genesis 33:19. Joseph was sold by his brothers for twenty shekels of silver in Genesis 37:28. Joseph's brother took silver to Egypt to buy food during the famine as recorded in Genesis Chapter 42.

It was obvious in the time of Jesus that even Matthew, the tax collector, collected money. Judas sold Jesus for money. Businessmen in ancient times had to be able to pay for services and goods with money, as well as to be able to barter.

To summarize, money was used frequently in ancient times. Some forms of money listed in the Bible are *talent, mina, shekel, mite, daric, denarius.* There are many others. Also, remember Jesus designated a man to carry His purse. What was in the purse? Money!

The tithe was known to be the Lord's property even while it was still growing in the field. In ancient times, the farmer could buy his tithe back from the Lord by paying the priest 120% of its value in money. The priest, in turn, would give the tithe (produce) back to the farmer and take the money and then buy a replacement tithe. Money was used, but never as a substitute for a tithe. The priests would never present money to the Lord, since His tithe was to be holy to Him and money was not (Leviticus 27:30). It must be remembered that the biblical definition of a tithe included what the tithe was composed of, which was agriculture products only.

INVESTIGATE TITHING

Most Christians are literate. They have Bibles, computers with Bible software, and volumes of biblical research books. Many have access to the Internet with its multitude of reports on just about every subject known to man. It is our responsibility to search out truth. This responsibility pertains not only to salvation, but also to giving. More than ever, Christians today must question and verify by the Scriptures what is being taught to them by ministers in the name of God. In my study of the Bible, concerning the principle of tithing, I reviewed the Scriptures and asked myself, "Was I was obeying God or Man?"

If you, the giver, want to pay tithes just because you have always paid tithes, then you should ensure that your tithes go where the Lord directed them under the Law, or you will have no guarantee of a blessing. Are your tithes going to feed strangers, the fatherless and the widows? Have you received your church's financial statements? You might be surprised at what you find.

The utilization of the tithe under the Law was a multi-faceted process. It was not as simple as everyone giving a tenth of his income to the ministry to be distributed at the discretion of the minister. Yet, that is the way the tithe is often taught in churches today. Many congregations are instructed to give 10% of their income (tithe) to the pastor as well as provide additional funds as necessary for other ministries (building funds, missionaries, education, etc.). What the pastors and church leaders do with the 10% tithe is totally at their discretion (in most cases). If tithing is going to be preached as a New Testament requirement, why aren't the distributions of the tithe preached with equal conviction? Why one without the other? Why the tithe, but not the proper utilization of the tithe? As taught in the Old Testament the proper utilization of the tithes was for the Levites, the widows, the fatherless, and the alien (stranger). My point is that the tithe should not be taught at all in our churches! The Lord established a marvelous giving plan for Christians as you will read later in this study.

CHAPTER SEVEN

The New Testament Church

We know that the new covenant is based on faith, which is motivated by love (Galatians 5:6). It is not based on strict adherence to the Law. Jesus came to fulfill the Law so that our relationship with God might be demonstrated through acts of love, not duty. It stands to reason that if our salvation is by faith through grace, then our giving would come under the same covering of love, grace, and faith. Why should finances come under the Law when everything else is under grace? We should study the gospels to see what Jesus had to say about giving and tithing. He said that He did not come to condemn the world, but that through Him, the world might be saved. Under the Law, if a person disobeyed one law, he was guilty of disobeying the entire Law, and was condemned. This is why we needed grace, God's unmerited favor. If Jesus had another method of dealing with sin, which is grace; then it stands to reason He has another method of dealing with finances. Wouldn't that be under grace as well?

WHERE DID NEW TESTAMENT TITHING ORIGINATE?

The New Testament church never paid tithes. Tithing was for the state of Israel, a taxation to support the priesthood of the Old Law of Moses. Christians never tithed until the Catholic Church came up with a plan at the Council of Macon in 585 A.D. The church needed a plan to take control of the money of the congregation. Due to covetousness, they brought people back under the Old Law to control them and their money (more regarding this in Chapter 11). The writer of Hebrews said that tithes were under the Law in Hebrews 7:5. *And verily they that are of the sons of Levi, who receive the office of the priesthood, have a commandment to take **tithes** of the people **according to the law**, that is, of their brethren, though they come out of the loins of Abraham.*

JESUS AND THE TITHE

Up to this point in our study, there are two scriptures with which I have not dealt. They are Matthew 23:23 and Luke 18:12. First, let's read Matthew 23:23. Jesus said, *"Woe to you, teachers of the law and Pharisees, you hypocrites! You give a tenth of your spices— mint, dill and cummin. But you have neglected the more important matters of the law— justice, mercy and faithfulness. You should have practiced the latter, without neglecting the former"* (*NIV*). We will see that Jesus' purpose was to condemn the attitudes and motives of the Pharisees. He did not appear to approve of the fact that they tithed on their spices, which was not required, as we will see.

In Jesus' generation, tithing was still imposed as a Levitical Law for those Jews under the first covenant (Matthew 23:23). The Temple was still in existence. The Levites and priests were still performing their occupation and were still the "legal" recipients of the agricultural tithe.

In different times during His earthly ministry, Jesus

appeared to back up the Mosaic government in the following areas:

- The temple tax (Matthew 17:24-27)
- Animal sacrifices and Levitical rituals (Matthew
  8:4; Mark 1:44; Luke 5:14)
- The authority of the scribes and Pharisees with
  respect to the *"seat of Moses"* (Matthew 23:2-3)

It is important to realize here that devout Jews made a point
of fasting on Mondays and Thursdays—according to their traditions, not according to the Law of God (Bock, *Luke*, [Baker
Books: 1996], p 1463). The Levitical Law required only crops
and animals to be tithed (Deuteronomy 24:22), but
Pharisees—according to *Talmudic Law*—tithed even on their
garden herbs (Bruce, *New Testament History*; p 72). Thus,
Jesus rebuked them for tithing their spices, mint, dill and
cummin. Jesus did not condemn them for their payment of
tithes, for they, in all probability, believed they should do so
according to the traditions they claimed were from their
fathers. In other words, He said in so many words that, the
problem is not that you tithe more than the Law requires. The
problem is that you omit the weightier matters of the Law,
such as justice, mercy, and faithfulness. It was their attitudes
and motives with which He took issue, not their tithing.

The Levitical system was still operative (for the temple
still stood), but they had diluted and polluted much of the
mandates dictated from God to Moses. Jesus' censure is
inherent in His condemnation of their hypocrisy. They were
as legalistic in their application of the tithing rules, as they
were in other aspects of their religious practices.

The Pharisee's obligation to pay the complete tithe meant
that he had to tithe what he ate, what he sold, and what he
bought. The Pharisees were tithe-payers *par excellence*
according to their oral laws, but *not* according to the laws of

the Old Testament. The Pharisee in Luke 18:12 could there-fore claim, *I give tithe of all that I possess.* He could *not* claim that the Law demanded this. Only their oral interpreta-tions of the Law demanded this. They wanted to go above even what the Scriptures demanded (Deuteronomy 14:23, for instance).

Where forms of religion or church policies are followed rather than Scripture, then matters of Scripture are annulled. This is a major problem in the Church. The ideas of men can often supersede application of Scripture. As noted, Pharisees tithed on the smallest of garden herbs and seeds, not because it was required of them, but because it was in keeping with the rabbinical ideas later *codified* in the Talmud. Yet the laws of offerings, sacrifices, and tithes, as given to Moses, were apparently upheld by Jesus *(These you ought to have done,* as God defines), for the temple still stood, the Pharisees *sat* in Moses' seat (Matthew 23:2-3), and they were obligated to *observe their own rulings.* However, endorsement of tithing is on Jesus' terms, not on the Pharisees'.

A REVIEW OF MATTHEW 23:23-34
AND LUKE 11:41-42

By their scrupulous attention to the physical, in this case, the tithing on the smallest of garden herbs, Jesus described the Pharisees as ***straining out a gnat.*** This was in reference to their practice of straining out their water so they would not accidentally swallow a gnat, which was an unclean insect according to the Law. It was indeed laid down in the Law that a gnat was an unclean insect, but the point Jesus was making was that the Pharisees were unbalanced in their strict, legalistic application of the letter of the Law, to the detriment of its spiritual intent, its *weightier matters.* He condemned their attitudes and motives, not their actions.

As Christians, we must analyze our lives to determine whether we have a balanced approach to New Testament teaching. Christian principles are not offered in a spiritual salad bar, in that we pick and choose. Either we believe the New Testament in its entirety and conform to its instructions, or we do not. It has been said that we will obey only those biblical principles we truly believe. In other words, if we are not conforming to them, then we do not really believe them.

Yes, the Levitical Law of the tithe was still operative. Jesus did not dismiss their devotion. He did deal with their double standards; the added implication is that their tithing law was a "gnat" in comparison with the weightier considerations of the Law. That is, it was of negligible importance when contrasted with God's great law of love. He positively took no pains to support it as having an ongoing worldwide purpose. He could easily have given further details about the subject, either here or elsewhere, but there is no record of such. If we look at the corresponding verses in Luke 11:41-42, we notice that He commended the spiritual kindness of the heart and the giving of alms over tithe paying (Matthew 6:1-4; 19:20-22). Jesus was encouraging them to let their hearts decide their generosity. This is a reflection of the *love of God,* rather than the requirement of tithing.

JESUS AND FINANCIAL STEWARDSHIP

History of Tithing from the Bible by Hubert Krause and Orest Solyma stated the following: "Jesus had many discussions with respect to financial matters and economic stewardship. Never once did He indicate that He or His disciples were to be the beneficiaries of the Levitical tithe in the future. Nor did He indicate that the Levitical tithe was compulsory for the Christian. He never indicated that the New Testament church would be financed by tithes.

The actuality is that Jesus could not legally have accepted tithes, because He was of the tribe of Judah. He was not a Levite and only the Levites and priests were permitted to accept offerings and tithes."

There is no evidence that Jesus ever collected tithes. He could have when he fed at least five thousand people. After all, the larger the gathering of people the greater amount of money that can be collected. Jesus could have collected a tithe to pay a temple tax, but He commanded a fish to provide the shekel for the temple tax instead (Matthew 17:24-27). Think about this: even though Jesus never received tithes, He managed to establish a ministry that has lasted over 2,000 years. How much money is really needed to start and maintain a church?

Please note these simple principles of Jesus:

- Matthew 10:8: Freely you have received, freely give, is the message of Christ.
- Matthew 19:21: The rich young man was to sell what he had and give to the poor, not to give to the temple or to the Levitical priesthood still functioning. This extraordinary order is restated in Mark 10:21 and Luke 18:22.
- Matthew 6:2-4: Jesus said that believers were to, **give alms, to help the poor and disadvantaged.**
- Luke 6:38: *Give, and it will be given to you: good measure, pressed down, shaken together, and running over will be put into your bosom. For with the same measure that you use, it will be measured back to you.*

Give compassionately, generously, voluntarily, and wisely, but not because you are under coercion. If you read this passage further, you will see that the subject concerns giving to the poor, not paying tithes.

In Acts 20:35, Luke records one of the great sayings of Jesus that is not mentioned anywhere else: **It is more blessed to give than to receive.** This statement comes from the context of **giving to the poor, not tithing.**

The Lord can hardly approve of paying a tithe out of feelings of guilt, fear, emotion, compulsion, coercion, or superstition. Jesus used the expression *give*. **A gift is not a debt coupled with the stigma of dishonor if it is not paid. A gift is offered freely as every man *purposes* in his heart.** Some believe that if they faithfully pay tithes, they will be given special material blessings. The Bible does not guarantee these blessings. However, giving to the poor does guarantee financial blessings.

TRADITION OR TRUTH

Some teach that the tithe is God's money and the church leaders are God's stewards, and those leaders will find the proper use for the money. As mentioned earlier, some churches even teach that once the tithe is given, one should not question how the money is spent. After all, it is now in the Lord's hands, so they say. Typically, in most churches, the tithe helps defray operating costs, building costs, and the various ministries. Some pastors, however, claim the entire tithe as their personal income. We have already seen that the Scriptures tell us that the priest only received a tithe of the tithe, or 10% of the whole tithe, not 100%.

Is it any wonder that paying tithes has become an accepted doctrine in some churches? It incites fear, finger pointing and intimidation. Who, after all, wants his or her Christian life questioned?

Some supposedly learned theologians, over many years, have completely misused the Old Testament tithing scriptures, and converted selected parts into a NEW binding law or duty which was never God-given or intended for the Church. Are we tithing based upon tradition or truth? If we tithe based on tradition, how different does that make us from the Pharisees who wrote and followed their Talmudic Law to the "nth degree?" As Christians, we already know that our harmony with God centers on grace through Jesus, not man-made laws or duties. **We are to walk in the Spirit and give by grace out of love, not duty.** Tithing out of duty is as unscriptural as salvation earned by good works. I call this "performance salvation."

PERFORMANCE SALVATION

Many groups teach performance salvation. Performance salvation negates the sacrifice made by our Lord and Savior on the cross. This "broken cross" message, preached by grace-killing, people-pleasing individuals, has again elevated law above grace. One of the most deceptive tools used to promote performance salvation is the man-made dogma of tithing for present day Christians.

Some teach that a consequence of not tithing is that it prevents the Lord from blessing you in many areas of your life. Let me ask you a question. If a church organization collects money in the name of a tithe and does not follow all the guidelines of tithing as set forth by the Lord, (i.e., giving all the tithe to the poor on the 3rd and 6th year of the Shemittah Cycle, observing the 7th year sabbatical and therefore not require a tithe, and allows the one who tithes to partake in the eating of the tithe in the presence of the Lord at the place of the Lord's choosing) then who is, according to the Law of Moses, really robbing God? The church organization and the ministers, and not the people! Refer back to Malachi 3: 6-12. Perhaps these verses are as applicable today as they were over 2,000 years ago.

WHAT DID JESUS TEACH ABOUT TITHING?

The main new covenant Scripture that many seem to use to justify tithing for Christians is Mark 12:41-44. This was the story of the widow giving two small coins. Jesus was in the temple sitting not far from where people were placing their money. Jesus was not counting their individual offerings. He was looking at the hearts of those who gave. A widow gave a very small amount, less than anyone else. Jesus said she gave *more* than everyone else! The small amount she gave was more valuable to the kingdom of God and to her, than all those who gave very large amounts. She certainly did not tithe. Instead, she gave all she had. Is Jesus saying that everyone should give all that they have? I don't think so, but we should be willing to give all. I believe we can learn the following lessons here: 1.) Just because you tithe doesn't mean you are pleasing God, 2.) If you are in a similar position as the widow then you could benefit by doing the same as the widow did, and 3.) God knows your giving and your heart.

God does not really need our money, but we need to give to Him. Remember, it is more blessed to give than to receive. It is for our good that we are commanded to give. Jesus said in Matthew 6:21 that where our treasure is, there will our heart be also. If we cannot give freely of our earthly monetary treasure, then how can we freely give God our heart? Perhaps God is aware that it would be impossible.

In Matthew 19:16-26, a rich young man asked Jesus a question about giving. This young man said he had obeyed all the laws, which included tithing. This young man wanted to know the one thing he had to do to achieve eternal life. Jesus saw through his question and went directly to the root of the problem; the young man loved his riches above everything else and he wanted to hold onto them. In other words, God knew his heart. The answer for the young man's problem was not tithing. Jesus said that the rich young man needed to sell all his possessions, give the money to the poor, and follow Him (Jesus). This was a test of the man's heart and perhaps the only way for him to get rid of his great love of money. If he had passed that test, maybe God could have blessed him with more riches than he had given away.

What does this mean to us? Is Jesus saying that everyone

should give all they have to the poor? Again, I don't think so. God promised us riches on this earth, so it is alright that Christians have money and valuables. It becomes a problem when having riches becomes the most important thing for us. Those who have the same dilemma as the rich young man, who trust in their riches more than they trust in God, need to take the same action Jesus recommended for the rich young ruler. It will show where their heart is.

One can store up memorials in heaven by giving to the poor as we see in Acts Chapter 10:4. As you will read in the next chapter, Cornelius was told twice that he had memorials in heaven for giving alms. Just because you faithfully tithe is no indication of God's acceptance of it. The Scripture is clear, however, that God readily accepts the giving of alms to the poor. Not only does He accept it, He memorializes it! Tithing may help keep the local church operating, but do not take comfort in that. We are told in Matthew Chapter 7:21-27 that although many people will do a whole lot better than just tithe, even they will not enter the kingdom of heaven.

The new covenant is based on faith that is motivated by love (Galatians 5:6), not adherence to the Law. The central theme of our salvation is faith, grace, and love, not the Law. Why should finances come under the Law when everything else is under grace? New Testament teaching concerning giving centers on the motive of one's heart, not the amount he gives. *Each man should give what he has decided in his heart to give, not reluctantly or under compulsion, for God loves a cheerful giver* (2 Corinthians 9:7). God does not receive glory if He has to coerce us to give as He did under the Law. He wants us to give freely to show our love for Him. This is the central theme of New Testament giving.

The chance of anyone proving that tithing was a New Testament practice is none, zilch, zip, and zero! (Johnson, R., *Lie of the Tithe*, page 167).

CHAPTER EIGHT

Church and Temple

A study of the New Testament quickly reveals that in the matters of financing the church and the spreading of the Gospel, there was no confusion or misunderstanding in the minds of the members of the apostolic church. No wonder, then, that we do not find detailed or elaborate debates on this subject in the New Testament. There seems to have been no need for debates, as we will clearly see from the Scriptures. In an attempt to prove that tithing is required today, some claim that during the period 30 to 70 A.D. the Levitical Law of tithing was automatically transferred to the New Testament Church. This application is obviously unprovable. Where, and when, and by what divine directive did this change take place? And why did the giving product of tithes change from agricultural items to money? Why not meat and drink offerings, as of old? Those who preach tithing do not feel comfortable with such questions.

The first-century, landowning Jew, who was called into the Church, was no longer required to obey the Levitical system. Why should the Levitical tithe alone be carried over to the church, as some would have us believe, when circumcision, rituals, and various specified offerings were erased from Christian practice?

Moreover, if a transfer of the Levitical tithe to the church did occur, which it didn't, how and when was the agricultural tithe suddenly converted into a money levy? The tithe of Israel was always agriculture products and only converted to money when travel requirements warranted it (Deuteronomy 14:24-26). Even then, the tithe-offerings made in the temple/tabernacle were food and offerings.

THE EARLY CHURCH

In 70 A.D. the temple was destroyed. Therefore, the need to provide for and sustain the Levites in their temple duties ceased. Although the New Testament church began forty years earlier, there is no evidence that Jesus or the apostles, even before 70 A.D., authorized any change in the Old Covenant Law. Like Jesus, the early church did not receive, nor could have received, the tithes. It was not entitled to these Levitical tithes, as by definition, as they belonged to the Levites. Jesus understood that. The right of the Levites and priests was not automatically the privilege of the ordained servants and shepherds of the spiritual Temple! All the children of God now came under a new agreement as driven by the Spirit.

There is no indication that Old Testament prophets received support from tithes. Furthermore, the Gospel did not, and does not today revolve around the service of the Levites in the temple. The Christian church is likewise not governed by the physical rituals associated with the temple services in Jerusalem. At the same time, we have the responsibility of supporting our pastors and those who give their lives to total service of the spiritual needs of believers. What method has God ordained for supplying this need?

Prior to 70 A.D., there is no indication that the early church, after Jesus' death and resurrection, made any claims on the Levitical tithes. Nor was there a requirement recorded that demanded tithing obligations upon its followers. Neither is there evidence in the New Testament or in early church history, that the tithing system of the Old Testament was used to support the new church.

The Gospel was carried forth by the power and the Spirit of God. It was not accomplished by the power of a group, or by the pooling of human resources and money into centralized control.

The church was growing by the thousands. Tithes were not collected. Yet, the early Christians, as recorded in Acts 4:32-37, sold land and possessions to help meet immediate physical needs. There is no reference here to tithe for any need.

Acts 5:4 summarizes divine retribution upon Ananias and his wife, who were corrupt to the trust and simplicity that characterized the beginning church. This couple sought recognition and prestige from supposedly very generous donations to the church. The reason their lives were taken is because they lied about how much they sold their property for, not for how much they gave.

GIVING STANDARDS IN THE EARLY CHURCH

The following standards were used in the early church as Hubert Krause and Orest Solyma record in *History of Tithing from the Bible*.

- **1 Corinthians 4:12,** *KJ21***:** And we labor, working with our own hands. Being reviled, we bless; being persecuted, we endure it.
- **2 Corinthians 11:7-9,** *NKJV***:** *Did I commit sin in humbling myself that you might be exalted, because I preached the Gospel of God to you free of charge? I robbed other churches, taking wages from them to minister to you. And when I was present with you, and in need, I was a burden to no one, for what I lacked the brethren who came from Macedonia supplied. And in*

*everything I kept myself from being burdensome
to you, and so I will keep myself.*

If the Corinthians, as some claim, were expected to tithe
to Paul in the Old Testament manner, then Paul would be
seen as forcing them to break that law by refusing to receive
their tithe. If a tithing law was indeed operative, and the
Corinthians were expected to give ten percent of their
income to the church and to the ministry, Paul would not
have stated that he was "robbing" them. He would surely
have been receiving what they *owed* him. His language does
not suggest that they were breaking an Old Testament tithing
law. *Those who preach the Gospel of God should be supported by those who hear and receive the Gospel.*

- **1 Thessalonians 2:8-12,** NKJV: *So, affectionately
  longing for you, we were well pleased to impart
  to you not only the Gospel of God, but also our
  own lives, because you had become dear to us.
  For you remember, brethren, our labor and toil;
  for laboring night and day, that we might not be
  a burden to any of you, we preached to you the
  Gospel of God. You are witnesses, and God also,
  how devoutly and justly and blamelessly we
  behaved ourselves among you who believe; as
  you know how we exhorted, and comforted, and
  charged every one of you, as a father does his
  own children, that you would walk worthy of God
  who calls you into His own Kingdom and glory.*
- **Philippians 4:15-19,** NKJV: *Now you Philippians
  know also that in the beginning of the Gospel* [first
  brought to the house of Lydia (Acts 16:12-15),
  who supported Paul], *when I departed from
  Macedonia, no* [other] *church shared with me concerning giving and receiving but you only. For*

*even in Thessalonica you sent aid once and again
for my necessities. Not that I seek the gift, but I
seek the fruit that abounds to your account. Indeed
I have all and abound. I am full, having received
from Epaphroditus the things sent from you, a
sweet-smelling aroma, an acceptable sacrifice,
well pleasing to God* [Paul praises and compares
this help to the sweet aroma from the sacrifices,
not the obedience of some supposed regulation].
*And my God shall supply all your need according
to His riches in glory by Jesus.*

DUAL GIVING SYSTEM IN FORCE

There were two separate systems operating during the
early church period. 1.) The Levitical priests were still serving in the temple. 2.) The New Testament ministry preaching
of the Gospel was an entirely separate entity. The Levitical
tithing practices were not transferred over to the New
Testament church to finance the ministry. The ministry of the
new covenant supersedes that of the Levitical ministry of the
previous covenant. Jesus authorized no transference of the
Levitical tithe to the New Testament ministry. However, the
two systems coexisted until about 70 A.D. Paul proclaimed
that an individual could only belong to one of the two, either
the church or the temple.

Paul talks about the Levites/priests eating the food and
sacrifices brought to the temple and to the altar. Some try to
legitimize the tithing system for the church today. The argument is often used that just as the tithes supported the
Levites and priests then, so they should support the ministry
today. If that is the case forget giving money and bring a cow
to the altar.

By and large, the Levitical priests were to be supported by
a system of offerings (Numbers 18:8-20) made on a regular
basis. These offerings were:

- Sin offerings
- Guilt offerings
- Devoted offerings
- Holy gifts and heave offerings
- Grain offerings
- Wave offerings
- First fruits and the best of the oil and wine

The priests received their ointment from a number of sources. Sin-offerings and reparation-offerings were normally their prerequisites. So were a considerable part of the cereal offerings, the shewbread, the breast and right shoulder of thank-offerings, the skins of the animals sacrificed as burnt-offerings, the first-fruits of grain and other produce of the earth (*terumah*) and of dough (*hallah*), the firstborn of cattle (or the money equivalent), the five shekels ransom money for human firstborn, part of the proceeds of sheep-shearing and a large number of occasional dues. The tithe (a ten percent income tax) was allotted mainly to the Levites, the non-priestly temple servants; <u>they paid one tenth of it to the priests.</u> The tithe of Deuteronomy (14:22; 26:12) was at this time interpreted as a second tithe (which it was not originally), to be expended on animals slaughtered for ordinary use (as distinct from those slaughtered for sacrifice), of which the priests received certain portions (Deuteronomy 18:3) (F.F. Bruce, *New Testament History*; p. 142).

THE LAW AND THE SPIRIT

God does not require Christians to conform to the tithing laws just as He does not require them to pay a temple tax! From around 70 A.D., the need for the agricultural tithe to feed the Levites in their rotation passed away. Even the Jews today do not tithe according to the first covenant laws for these same reasons.

Jesus and His disciples provided for their festival needs

from everyday expenses (John 13:29). There is no Scripture in the entire New Testament to indicate that the early Christian leaders ever taught tithing, as a means of funding for the keeping of the festivals, or for any other purpose, for that matter.

The method used by the early church to support itself and its work is the method Christians should employ today. God's Spirit convicts the Christian to give according to his heart, as a *cheerful giver* (2 Corinthians 9:7), giving *not as of necessity, but willingly* (Philemon 14), ... *so that any favor you do will be spontaneous and not forced,* not according to prescribed limits laid down by some sort of "law," but as convicted by the Holy Spirit.

The tithe is used as a legal requirement for Christians today. It becomes a religious standard by which to measure oneself, and/or a ceiling for giving. Yet, the biblical declaration is simply to give with openhandedness (Romans 12:8), ... *Let him give generously,* which may at times exceed any defined limits and system standards. Giving should not be a requirement based on a mathematical formula, but from the heart. One pastor told me that he could judge the spirituality of his saints by watching the tithing account! Into what kind of bondage does that put his congregation, knowing that he is looking at facts and figures to gauge their spirituality?

Many churches accept the tithe even if it is acknowledged to be non-binding upon the church today as a financial standard of giving. Where is the scriptural legality for turning Old Testament laws into current specific financial standards of giving?

We read in the following scriptures that Peter, Paul and Barnabas set the Pharisees straight about the Gentiles having to obey the Law of Moses. At this meeting it is stated loud and clear that the only laws that the Gentiles should obey are to abstain from food sacrificed to idols, from blood, from the meat of strangled animals and from sexual immorality. There

is nothing about the law of tithing listed here. Paul and
Barnabas said that God owned the preaching of the pure
gospel to the Gentiles without the Law of Moses; therefore to
press that law upon them was to undo what God had done.

*And certain men came down from Judea and
taught the brethren, Unless you are circumcised
according to the custom of Moses, you cannot be
saved ... but some of the sect of the Pharisees who
believed rose up, saying, "**It is necessary to cir-
cumcise them, and to command them to keep the
law of Moses.**" ... and when there had been much
dispute, Peter rose up and said to them: "Men and
brethren, you know that a good while ago God
chose among us, that by my mouth the Gentiles
should hear the word of the gospel and believe. So
God, who knows the heart, acknowledged them by
giving them the Holy Spirit, just as He did to us,
and made no distinction between us and them,
purifying their hearts by faith. **Now therefore, why
do you test God by putting a yoke on the neck of
the disciples which neither our fathers nor we
were able to bear?** But we believe that through the
grace of the Lord Jesus Christ we shall be saved in
the same manner as they...Therefore I judge that
we should not trouble those from among the
Gentiles who are turning to God, but that we write
to them to <u>abstain from things polluted by idols</u>,
from <u>sexual immorality</u>, from <u>things strangled, and
from blood</u>...you must be circumcised <u>and keep the
law</u>—to whom we gave no such commandment ...
For it seemed good to the Holy Spirit, and to us, to
lay upon you no greater burden than these necessary things: that you abstain from things offered to
idols, from blood, from things strangled, and from*

sexual immorality. If you keep yourselves from these, you will do well. Farewell" (Acts 15:5-29, NKJV).

We find another example of Paul getting very upset with those foolish Galatians. *Brothers, if I am still preaching circumcision, why am I still being persecuted? In that case the offense of the cross has been abolished. As for those agitators, I wish they would go the whole way and emasculate themselves!* (Galatians 5:11-12, NIV).

Paul gave them a choice if they wanted to demand circumcision and be under the law. I doubt than many wanted back under the Law when he told them to castrate themselves. Those strong words may be necessary to get the attention of some Christian leaders today.

Part III

CHAPTER NINE

Should New Testament Believers Tithe?

You have been presented with enough information to question what you have been taught. That is, if you have been taught like the majority of Christians today. Who am I, and why am I challenging a major tradition in the church? I am a grateful sinner who has been saved by the grace of Jesus! The Lord has given me a beautiful family, financial security, and the gift of giving. Jesus said that to whom much is given much is required. After my born-again experience, I wanted to give back to the work of the Lord as a token of my love and devotion to Him. Before I discovered the truth about tithing, I always tithed to my hometown church. I even tithed before I became a Christian because I was taught that as a child.

For many years I have given more than I could claim on my income tax return. My accountant is always amazed at the amount of contribution carryover I have each year. But, as I tell him and others, "You can't out-give the Lord." I am thankful to say that I give to many needy programs and I am blessed because of it, but I see others give generously and they are not blessed. What is the problem? We know that God does not lie.

He says, "Test Me ... Try Me ... Prove Me, and see if I will not bless you." There are no IOU's on God's desk. It is not God's fault if a Christian is not blessed even though he is a giver. God promised to bless the giver, so where is the problem? There is nothing wrong with God. And, because God's blessings are because of His love of mankind, and not based on our own righteousness, most likely there is nothing wrong with the giver. Something is wrong with the system. The fault lies in what we have been taught.

It is not easy to challenge the system. Leaders, especially pastors who are overburdened with church duties, cares, family matters, and the like, do not desire to be disputed. They want to leave well enough alone. Challengers are viewed as dissenters, rebels, and nonconformists; and so, they are labeled as such. The label is intended to warn other members to avoid these so-called troublemakers.

Can someone give to a religious group and think to himself, *I gave as unto the Lord. It is their responsibility to do the right thing with my gift. The Lord will give me credit for giving*? Anyone who thinks this way has missed the mark. There is no personal responsibility in this kind of thinking. Cain thought this way and it launched him into serious trouble with the Almighty! According to Genesis 4, the Lord rejected his sacrifice because Cain did not conform to God's directive.

The Dawson family who gave $400,000 was not blessed financially. Why? Because they and many others have been coached into obeying the commands of man rather than the commands of God!

I covered the commands of Jesus in Matthew 25 earlier, but this is such an important part of being a Christian I want to review it again. One day, shortly after becoming a Christian, I was playing "Bible Roulette." That is, I was shuffling through the pages of the Bible, praying that the Lord would show me something that I needed to know. My Bible stopped in Matthew at Chapter 25. What a shocking statement I discovered recorded on those pages! Jesus boldly stated that those who had not fed the hungry, clothe the naked, or visited the sick and imprisoned would be sent into everlasting punishment. Wow! I was devastated. According to Jesus, I was lost. I had paid tithes for years, but I had not obeyed those very firm and judgmental words of Jesus.

Make special note that those who obeyed Jesus on this issue were shocked that they were called righteous and surprised that they were saved. This judgment takes place on the last day, when the Son of Man comes in His glory. The last day is too late to correct error, because judgment is settled. Please read on.

I know of no way around this persuasive command of Jesus if we expect to be saved. It is so simple. We must feed the hungry, clothe the needy, care for the sick, and visit those who are incarcerated. Some poor souls will learn on the last day, when it is too late to correct their error, that they are lacking the necessary qualifications to escape everlasting punishment. Jesus said it, not I. Notice that He makes no mention of any requirement to pay tithes. Paying tithes is mentioned often in churches today (every service at offering time), this necessary salvation command of helping the needy is seldom preached to New Testament Christians. In most churches there is no special place on the tithing envelopes to check for feeding the hungry and clothing the needy. Why is this soul saving message overlooked?

RIGHTLY DIVIDING THE WORD OF TRUTH
My humble observation on current tithing requirements is presented only after years of study, hours of prayer on the subject, and talking with many fellow Christians who share similar concerns. I have paid tithes to Christian organizations for more than 50 years, because I was taught to do so. I never questioned whether tithing was a requirement for New Testament Christians. It was not until I read the Bible for

myself and made an authentic study on the topic of giving, that I discovered I had also been misinformed. As I stated earlier, I believe my spiritual leaders had been deceived. I believe that the tradition of tithing is a misinterpretation by many Christian leaders. Unfortunately, few people seek to discover truth. Some people seek out selective scriptures in order to confirm their errors and perpetuate their narrow-mindedness! An error does not become a mistake until we refuse to correct it. Now is the time to correct our thinking, believing, and acting concerning New Testament giving. The legalistic form of compulsory tithing was only commanded under the Law for farmers giving agriculture products. Even then, it was not taught the way it is taught in the Church today that require tithing on money.

Many unscriptural doctrines are taught because of misinterpretations of the Word of God. One can take a single scripture, without a witness from another scripture, and build a kingdom around it. If we only read that *Jesus wept,* without reading more about Him, we may conclude that he was only a crybaby. In addition to the tithing issue, we see this type of deception taught concerning baptism for the dead, drinking poison, playing with fire, handling snakes, and not playing musical instruments in the church. Yet, there are many scriptural witnesses for the perfect will of God throughout the Bible. We need to rightly divide the Word of truth, and not add to it.

Old Testament tithing in New Testament churches is nothing more than the lifting of scriptures out of context and modifying them to fit the need of those in control. If our salvation message is found in the New Testament, so should our giving requirements be taken from the New Testament. Tithing has been made a tradition to control New Testament Christians in the manner of giving. Over time, the tradition has become legitimized and has been perpetuated as truth. If one questions this tradition, he becomes a problem. He is labeled a "liberal" or given some other demeaning tag in hopes he will leave the congregation and not cause any problems. Sincere questioners are told that the leadership has divine authority and that they are not to be questioned. Since these leaders do not have a mandate from Scripture, they tend to guard these "sacred cows" not with love and tolerance, but with threatened excommunication to sincere seekers of truth. This is an abuse of power and authority.

The Word of God is the yardstick for modeling godly Christian behavior. It is therefore imperative that believers understand the Bible. Clear understanding and valid interpretation comes not only with respect to the literal translation, but also within the culture and historical setting of the writing. Interpretation must also be made with respect to God's plan for man's redemption, for this is the central theme of the New Testament. **Understanding the Scriptures requires study, not only of the Word itself, but also requires a questioning attitude**. This is not a self-righteous, arrogant attitude that questions the truth of the Bible. It is an individual who humbly seeks a better understanding and will always study and verify Scripture within the context in which it was written. It is therefore necessary to continually study the whole Bible in context. It cannot be done accurately through selective Scripture studies. A person who is well versed in the Scriptures will be able to test the words he hears from pastors, ministers and friends.

The Bible commands us to search the Scriptures (John 5:39). Sadly, some churches, having once had their roots in solid, biblical truth, have changed! They have evolved into modified gospels as a result of the infiltration of the traditions of men and cultural changes over the years. The Apostle Paul urged believers to, *Examine everything carefully, hold fast to that which is good* (1 Thessalonians 5:21, NAS). **It is your responsibility, as a Christian, to know how to test teachings. No one else will do this for you.** God will hold you accountable.

ROBBING GOD OF TITHES AND OFFERINGS
There is another issue regarding the doctrine of tithing that must be addressed. When this doctrine is taught in New Testament churches today, the Scripture in Malachi 3:8-9 is used to bring great conviction on the people if they are not faithful tithers.

> *Will a man rob God? Yet you have robbed Me. But you ask, "How do we rob You? In tithes and offerings. You are under a curse. The whole nation of you because you are robbing me"* (Malachi 3:8-9, NIV).

It is obvious that someone or something robbed God in tithes and offerings. But who? To get the correct answer to this question, we must look at the beginning of the book of Malachi and see to whom the charge was made. Malachi 1:6-8 tells us that the charge was presented to the priests, not to the Jewish community at large. Who was robbing God? Was it the people or the priests? If you read the entire book of Malachi you will see that God is addressing the priests, not the people.

In the first chapter of Malachi we see that the Lord is charging the priest with offerings, which are unacceptable for the altar.

> *"If I am a father, where is the honor due me? If I am a master, where is the respect due me?" says the LORD Almighty. "It is you, **O priests**, who show contempt for my name. But you ask, 'How have we shown contempt for your name?' You place defiled food on my altar. But you ask, 'How have we defiled you?' By saying that the LORD's table is*

contemptible. When you bring blind animals for sacrifice, is that not wrong? When you sacrifice crippled or diseased animals, is that not wrong? Try offering them to your governor! Would he be pleased with you? Would he accept you?" says the LORD *Almighty* (Malachi 1:6-8, *NIV*).

The second chapter of Malachi is addressed to the priest as well, *"And now this admonition is for you* **O priest***. If you do not listen, and if you do not set your heart to honor my name," says the Lord Almighty ... "But you have departed from the way; you have caused many to stumble at the law ..."* Chapter 3 is still addressing the priest, *"So I will come near to you for judgment. I will be quick to testify against sorcerers, adulterers and perjurers, against those who defraud laborers of their wages, who oppress the widows and the fatherless, and deprive the aliens of justice, but do not fear me," says the Lord Almighty* (Malachi 3:5, *NIV*).

The priest was the one who was responsible for the offerings, and therefore he was the one who received the reprimand. Malachi 3:8-9, which is commonly used to convince Christians they are cheating God if they do not tithe, was directed to the priest, not to the people.

How were the priests robbing God? As I have indicated above, the tithe was for Levite, the stranger, the fatherless and the widow. The unacceptable agriculture products and the defiled foods that were accepted by the priest (the tithe products) were an outrage to God. Since God is holy, He commanded the best from the people. These priests were robbing God of His glory. They could not rob Him of earthly goods because He owned everything. But they could rob Him of His majesty by not giving the best to the needy. I feel it is necessary to repeat how God addresses that problem in Malachi 3:5, *NIV "... I will be quick to testify against sorcerers, adulterers and perjurers, against those who defraud*

*laborers of their wages, <u>who oppress the widows and the</u>
<u>fatherless, and deprive the aliens of justice,</u> but do not fear
me," says the Lord Almighty.*

Jesus also addressed this type of robbery in the New
Testament in Matthew 25:42, *NIV, For I was hungry and you
gave me nothing to eat ... I tell you the truth, whatever you
did not do for one of the least of these, you did not do it for
me.* Yes, the priest robbed God by not feeding the needy as
Malachi recorded. They are still robbing Him today by not
taking care of the needy. I know of one church that has lim-
ited the amount of money for the benevolence ministry (the
poor and needy) to a pittance. Regardless of how much
comes in, the benevolence minister can only spend so much.
The reason? The church has other needs and the money is
distributed at the discretion of the ministers. In other words,
when money gets tight, the poor and needy are the ones who
suffer, not the organization. In many churches there has not
been any provisions made to help the needy. This is not
Christ-like!

Some pastors believe that 100% of the tithe belongs to
them and to their families. One pastor told me, "My stingy
saints did not put enough money in the offering plate to pay
the utility bill. I will have to take money out of my tithing
account to make up the difference." A man's judgment is no
better than his information.

I reviewed the financial statements of another church that
had an annual income of almost $2 million. I discovered
nearly $1.5 million was designated as tithes and kept by the
pastor. This salary was paid even while the church had difficulty paying the normal operating expenses! Less than .1%
of the $2 million was spent on helping the needy.

Something is seriously wrong. This is, without a doubt,
tradition and legalism in action. I am sure the pastors who
operate this way think that they are obeying God. If they
want to operate under the Law of Tithing then they should

ensure that the stranger, the fatherless and the widow get their portion.

Many churches that collect tithing, have no means to support the needy of their city or other needed programs. Instead, over-worked mothers hold an endless number of bake sales. In other words, church members are requested to give additional time and money after having already given over 10% of their incomes in tithes and offerings. It would be interesting to find out just how many pies, suckers and peanut brittle packages have been sold by Christian ladies across the country to build churches!

Paul had this to say concerning preachers pay. *Don't you know that those who work in the Temple get their meals from the food brought to the Temple as offerings? And those who serve at the altar get a share of the sacrificial offerings. In the same way, <u>the Lord gave orders that those who preach the Good News</u> should be supported by those who benefit from it. Yet I have never used any of these rights. And I am not writing this to suggest that I would like to start now. In fact, I would rather die than lose my distinction of preaching without charge. For preaching the Good News is not something I can boast about. I am compelled by God to do it. How terrible for me if I didn't do it!* (1 Corinthians 9:13-16, NLT).

Christians are clearly supposed to support those who preach and work in the ministry. However, Paul was willing to waive his rights to a material harvest rather than disrupt the work of God. Of course it would be very difficult for those who preach the Good News today to go without salaries and I am not suggesting that as a consideration. And as Paul says the Lord has given orders for the ministers to be supported, but please note he said nothing about collecting tithes for his labor. Some ministers can't seem to get enough compensation for preaching the Good News. For example a minister acquaintance of mine recently declared that he made $25,000 a week-end teaching seminars in churches across the nation. In fact he was bragging about the fact that he did not have to preach each week to live a very comfortable life. This is a far cry from the obligation that Paul took on free of charge.

We must support the five-fold ministry, but tithing is not the way to do it. If we could only get back to the biblical way of giving, then the giver would be blessed as well as the receiver. All the church's needs would be met, the ministers would be paid, and the poor would not be neglected. God's way works!

As we have noted thus far, tithing was commanded only for those who were in the agriculture business. Tithes consisted of food taken from the farms to be consumed in the temple or given to the poor. There were many other professions listed in the Bible that were non-agricultural, but there was no command for them to tithe. Following are just a few of such vocations: masons, stone cutters, musicians, tent makers, merchants, inn keepers, metal smiths, gold smiths, butchers, bakers, candlestick makers, carpenters, and tax collectors. There were many more professions other than farming that existed at that time that were not commanded to tithe.

In review, we note the tithe was to be an agricultural product, never money. The tithe was to be eaten by the priest and the people. If it was not consumed, it was to be burned. So, the tithe of the Old Testament was never money! Yet, today it takes money to run the church, pay the preachers, the missionaries, and feed and care for the poor. If tithing is not the biblical method of handling these needs, what is? The New Testament method is as complete and meticulous as the Old Testament method as you will read in this book.

WHAT OTHERS SAY ABOUT TITHING!

"The tithe as part of *the Law* is no more applica-

ble to us than making a pilgrimage to Jerusalem three times a year is. It is mentioned in the New Testament only a couple of times, generally in the context of *rebuke* to the Pharisees concerning fastidious observance of the ceremonial Law. If God had intended to carry *tithing* over into the new covenant, then the chance was missed in Acts 15. You will note tithing is not mentioned in the Acts 15 Jerusalem Council rulings; though for modern legalists this is a favorite extra-biblical 'exception' or 'carryover' from the old Covenant Law." **Dean VanDruff, Internet.**

"The absence of a command for tithing does not relieve Christians of the responsibility to give. Rather, Christians are held to the higher law of stewardship—acknowledging that everything we have is a gift from God and being willing to give it all at any moment that Christ commands (Matthew 19:21)." **Kevin Whitehead, Internet.**

"Christians should give of their time, money, and spiritual gifts as they determine in their own heart, and not be coerced into giving a set percentage of their income." **Dave Combs, Internet.**

"The tithe is erroneously applied to Christians by pulling the Old Testament law of tithing across dispensations and placing it as doctrine in the New Testament. This is how most false doctrines originate. When doctrines, which are valid in only one dispensation (time period), are forced into another dispensation they become false doctrines. For example, many preachers quote Malachi 3:10 (*Bring ye all the tithes into the storehouse, that there may be meat in mine house*) as if a New Testament church is the storehouse, but the church is never spoken of as a storehouse for God's goods. Churches were not intended to store crops and livestock (or even money) as the passage refers to. This is one area where otherwise sound and sensible preachers will spiritualize and compromise the Bible to promote their pet doctrines or traditional belief." **Timothy S. Morton, Internet.**

"God never authorized Christian leaders to take a tithe from God's people. One will not find the modern church tithe authorized in the old covenant, nor in the new covenant. Certainly, church historians are in agreement, when they say that the early believers did not practice tithing. The tithe as taught by most Christian denominations as being 10 per cent of gross or net income is not contained on the pages of the Bible!" **Gary Amirault, Internet.**

"Churches advocating tithing as compulsory are putting a **curse** on their congregations! So in summary, giving is a New Testament Church principal as opposed to tithing by Law." **Dr. Eddy Cheong, Internet.**

"The Jews are the only ones who were ever commanded to pay tithes. Many pastors terrify their people and threaten them with horrible judgments. They say, 'If you don't tithe, God will cause you to have sickness, doctor and hospital bills. If you don't pay that which belongs to God, you will have trouble, pestilence, loss of job, loss of money, poverty and other misfortunes.' To prove their point they open the Bible and read the Old

Testament Law in Malachi, and in the book of Deuteronomy. What pathetic jumbling of the Word of God!" **Dr. Charles Halff, Internet.**

My report was finished on tithing. I had spent hours on the subject and was about ready to put the finishing touches on the testimony. But, I asked the Lord in my way, "Is this report correct?" I again was impressed to try one more search on the Internet. Wow! I found volumes of additional information covering the subject of tithing. Hubert Krause taught tithing for more than 30 years to his Pentecostal church before he discovered the truth about true giving. I am thankful for this confirmation. Just use your search engine on the Internet and you will find volumes written about tithing.

CHAPTER TEN

More Guarantees

God wants to bless His children. We see His desire to do so conveyed repeatedly throughout the Scriptures. This blessing encompasses every area of our lives, including our health, our work, our relationships, and our finances. Since we are talking about finances and we have discovered that tithing is not the New Testament guarantee for coming under God's financial blessing, we need to know what is. To get an idea, consider the following promises.

- *Blessed is he who considers the poor; the Lord will deliver him in time of trouble* (Psalms.41:1).
- *He who has pity on the poor lends to the Lord, and He will pay back what he has given* (Proverbs 19:17, *NIV*).
- *He who has a generous eye will be blessed, for he gives of his bread to the poor* (Proverbs 22:9, *NKJV*).
- *A generous man will prosper; he who refreshes others will himself be refreshed* (Proverbs 11:25, *NIV*).

Even though these scriptures are in the Old Testament

they are relevant. Proverbs especially, is an excellent guideline for healthy, prosperous, wholesome living. So do not discount God's promises just because they are in the Old Testament. The only distinction to look for in determining whether an Old Testament promise applies to us or not, is whether it nullifies God's grace, because as Christians, we are under grace, not the Law (grace over-rules Law). If it is a promise with a condition and we meet the condition, we can count on the guarantee God makes.

The Bible teaches us that those who give to the poor can expect blessing, not from those to whom they give, but from God Himself. Each of the above verses is a promise with a guaranteed blessing. These guarantees can be counted on as surely as any other promise in the Bible. **If God's guarantees fail concerning giving to the poor, then we have the right to question the virgin birth, the resurrection, and the second coming of Jesus!** God esteems giving to the poor so highly that not only is He willing to bless us financially on earth, but He will memorialize our giving in heaven. As I wrote earlier in this book Cornelius gave to the poor and it was recorded in heaven. *One day at about three in the afternoon he had a vision. He distinctly saw an angel of God, who came to him and said, "Cornelius!" Cornelius stared at him in fear. "What is it, Lord?" he asked. The angel answered* ***"Your prayers and gifts to the poor have come up as a memorial before God"*** (Acts 10:3-4, *NIV*). Think of the great memorials we have all over this country, the World War II memorial in Pearl Harbor for the WW II veterans, the Viet Nam War Memorial in Washington, D. C., just to name two. Those memorials exist so that we will not forget the sacrifices that were made on our behalf and others. God thinks so highly of our sacrifice, that He will commemorate our prayers and giving of alms throughout all of eternity.

Now, let us consider two additional Bible teaching concerning giving (or the lack of it), to the poor:

- *He <u>who gives to the poor</u> will not lack, but he who hides his eyes will have many curses* (Proverbs 28:27, *NIV*).
- *Whoever shuts his ears to the cry of the poor will also cry himself and not be heard* (Proverbs 21:13, *NIV*).

When we take a long, hard look at all of the previously quoted verses, Malachi 3 can now be understood. God was telling the priests they were cursed because they robbed Him by not following His ordinances. He was telling them that they were robbing God because they had not fed the poor through the proper distribution of the tithe. In Deuteronomy Chapters 14 and 26, God speaks specifically about the portion of the tithes that goes into the storehouse, which was not only to feed the Levites, **but also to care for the poor.** So, part of the tithes belongs to the poor. If you pay tithes today make sure that part of that agricultual gift goes to the poor.

Deuteronomy 27:19 is another verse that demonstrates what God thinks about those who do not allow the poor their portion: *Cursed is the one who perverts the justice due the stranger, the fatherless, and widow.*

YOU DETERMINE YOUR BLESSINGS

Jesus explains in Luke 6:38 that we will be blessed in proportion **to how we bless others through our giving.** This teaching is repeated later in 2 Corinthians 9:6—if you give a little, you will be blessed a little. If you give a lot, you will be blessed a lot. Both of these scriptures are explaining the benefit of generosity. For some reason, many people associate tithing with being generous. **Tithing and generosity are not the same.** A person can tithe and still not be generous. He may only be obeying a law that he has been taught. Generosity is helping others voluntary. When one gives as an act of charity the result will bury our selfishness and develop a giving attitude, so much so that we begin to *love* to give! It must become our heartbeat just as it is the heartbeat of Jesus. This is being Christ like. It takes hard work to change our strong will. Tithing, on the other hand, is an attempt to please God and man by obeying an outdated law that was given to the Israelites.

NEW TESTAMENT PLAN FOR GIVING
The following verses are very interesting:

- *He who oppresses the poor to increase his riches, and he who gives to the rich, will surely come to poverty* (Proverbs 22:16, *NIV*).
- *If you want to be perfect, go, sell what you have and give TO THE POOR, and you will have treasure in heaven; and come, follow Me* (Matthew 19:21, *NIV*)
- *One thing thou lackest: go thy way, sell whatsoever thou hast, and give to the poor, and thou shalt have treasure in heaven: and come, take up the cross, and follow me* (Mark 10:21).
- *Now when Jesus heard these things, he said unto him, Yet lackest thou one thing: sell all that thou hast, and distribute unto the poor, and thou shalt have treasure in heaven: and come, follow me* (Luke 18:22).
- *Sell what you have and give alms ... provide yourselves a treasure in heaven ...*(Luke 12: 33-34, *NIV*).

The epistles concur with Jesus' teachings regarding giving. The first incident we will study is found in Acts: *Now the whole group of believers was one in heart and soul, and nobody called any of his possessions his own. Instead, they shared everything they owned. With great power the apostles continued to testify to the resurrection of the Lord Jesus, and abundant grace was on them all. For none of them needed anything, because all who had land or houses would sell them and bring the money received for the things sold and lay it at the apostles' feet. Then it was distributed to anyone who needed it. Now Joseph, a Levite and a native of Cyprus, who was named Barnabas by the apostles (which means a son of encouragement), sold a field that belonged to him and brought the money and laid it at the apostles' feet* (Acts 4:32-37, *NKJV*).

There is a lot to be learned from these passages. The believers were in agreement, and sharing was common. The apostles were teaching about the resurrection of Jesus with great power and much grace was upon them. They were free, just as we are, to give what they wanted to give.

In 1 Corinthians 16:1-3, Paul instructed the believers to "set aside a sum of money in keeping with his income" as they prepared to raise money for the believers in Jerusalem. It seems as though many interpret this as some kind of code word for tithing. It is not. It simply means that you, the giver, are free to decide how much money is in keeping with your income and you give that amount. Paul is not instructing believers to tithe. *Now concerning the collection for the saints, as I have given orders to the churches of Galatia, so you must do also: On the first day of the week let each one of you lay something aside, storing up as he may prosper, that there be no collections when I come. And when I come, whomever you approve by your letters I will send to bear your gift to Jerusalem* (1 Corinthians 16:1-3, *NKJV*). *Something* is not a tithe; it is a sum, not a specific amount, not 10%!

The most significant text concerning generosity in the epistles is recorded in 2 Corinthians Chapter 8 and continues through to 2 Corinthians Chapter 9. Again, there is much more contained in these scriptures than what we will cover here. Paul first writes about *the grace that God has given the Macedonian churches* as he referred to their *rich generosity*. In verse 7, Paul encouraged the Corinthian church and believers today to see *that you also excel in this grace of giving*. These are not code words for tithing. It means that God has provided His grace to us so that we may be generous to those in need.

The generous Macedonian church was not rich at all. In fact Paul wrote in verse 2, ... *their overflowing joy and their extreme poverty welled up in rich generosity*. Once again, it is the condition of their hearts that mattered more than the amount they gave. Believers need to search their own hearts and give what they are really happy to give, no more, or no less.

Are the churches that use Scripture to enforce collection of money in the name of tithes opening themselves up to judgment? When observing the Law, all of the Law must be observed, not just the parts that are of benefit to the church and pastors. Christians must not have a pick and choose mentality when it comes to the Word of God. According to the Law, if those churches do not follow the Scriptures concerning the *distribution* of the tithes as well as the *collection* of the tithes, then they are bringing judgment upon themselves.

This study is not intended to discourage churches from obtaining necessary financial support. Churches have many good ministries worthy of support and should encourage their members to actively participate financially in three areas: 1.) The church itself, including all operating costs, 2.) The ministries for worship of our Lord and 3.) For the aid of the needy, thus revealing Jesus in us. According to the Scriptures, this last area is more important than the others. If it is adhered to generously, there will be more than enough for every good work, including the support of the ministers and the local church.

The purpose of this study is to confront the abuse of Scripture in the modern church and resulting methods used to collect money in the name of God. God wants the new covenant church to walk in the freedom of the Spirit (Galatians 5:16). *Now the Lord is the Spirit, and where the Spirit of the Lord is, there is freedom* (2 Corinthians 3:17, *NIV*). A portion of this freedom is the choice of participating in and expressing the love and joy of true giving.

GIVING THAT GOD LOVES MOST

I examined hundreds of references in the Bible in order to find which method of giving God loves most. One does not have to be a skilled statistician to quickly conclude that **God addresses giving to the needy more** often than He addresses all other forms of giving combined. I have noted only a few of the many scriptures on helping the poor and needy in this study. I challenge you to do your own study on that subject in the Bible and make special note of the guarantees that come with giving to the poor.

God is not looking for people to tithe. God wants His people to obey Him as He speaks to their hearts. He is looking for co-laborers, partners in life who will join their hearts with His to accomplish His will on earth. Each believer is accountable to the Lord for his obedience to the Holy Spirit. Search your own heart and determine the amount you can freely give, and then give it cheerfully as unto the Lord. By doing this, He guarantees you a spiritual and financial blessing as well.

Let me give you an example. Some time ago I was blessed by selling some real estate. I wanted to be a blessing to someone else, so I asked the Lord to show me where the money should go. In a matter of moments the name Daily Bread flashed through my mind. I knew this was the Lord speaking to me. Many people struggle with these kinds of thoughts and wonder *was that the Lord or was it me?* I knew it was not my own idea because of what God said in Proverbs 16:3 in the *Amplified Bible. Roll your works upon the Lord—commit and trust them wholly to Him; [He will cause your thoughts to become agreeable to His will, and] so shall your plans be established and succeed.* I had asked the Lord to direct me and He caused my thoughts to agree with His will.

Daily Bread is a ministry that has been feeding and clothing the needy for many years on the streets of my city. Not only do they attend to their physical need of the needy, but to their spiritual need as well. I had not thought of this ministry in a long time, but God knew all about their mission. I am so thankful that He let me know where to give. I was abundantly blessed once again for following His leadership.

Do you see the difference between giving under compulsion and giving cheerfully? The tithe, as a component of the Mosaic Law, which was never reinstated as part of the teaching of Jesus or the apostles, does not apply to Christians.

"While not requiring a tithe of believers today, the New Testament does speak of God's blessing on those who give generously to the needs of the church and especially to those who labor in the Word." *(The Bible Knowledge Commentary: Old Testament, John F. Walvoord, Roy B. Zuck, p. 1585.)*

"Tithing is not taught in the New Testament as an obligation for the Christian under grace ... because we are not under law, but under grace. Christian giving must not be made a matter of legalistic obligation, lest we fall into the error of Galatianism ...." *(The New Treasury of Scripture Knowledge,* Jerome Smith, p. 1152).

Could we be displeasing God by our tithing? Remember how angry God was when Saul offered the sacrifice instead of waiting for the prophet Samuel to perform the function as was commanded? Yes, the offering was sacrificed on the altar, but it was not according to God's commandments. We may be giving money to the church, but is it as God commands? It is impossible to please God without faith (Hebrews 11:6). How can we truly do anything by faith if it is not in compliance with His commands? The Church needs to answer these questions. If she does not, she will be guilty of neglecting her responsibilities to the saints of God.

The absence of a command for tithing does not relieve Christians of the responsibility to give. Rather, Christians are held to the higher law of stewardship—acknowledging that everything we have is a gift from God, and being willing to give it all up at any moment that Jesus commands (Matthew 19:21).

The Bible specifies two main reasons for Christian giving. First, Christians should provide for the needs of fellow Christians who are experiencing financial hardships. For example, while Barnabas and Saul were ministering in Antioch, ... *some prophets came down from Jerusalem to Antioch. One of them, named Agabus, stood up and through the Spirit predicted that a severe famine would spread over the entire Roman world. The disciples, each according to his own ability, decided to provide help for the brothers living in Judea. This they did, sending their gift to the elders by Barnabas and Saul* (Acts 11:27-30, *NIV*).

Paul gave instruction to churches that they should give to the poor Christians in Jerusalem. ... *Macedonia and Achaia were pleased to make a <u>contribution for the poor</u> among the saints in Jerusalem* (Romans 15:26, *NIV*). Christians should follow these examples and provide for the needs of our brothers and sisters in Christ who are in financial distress.

A second reason for Christian giving is to support Christian leaders. Paul wrote to the Corinthians that ... <u>*those who preach the gospel should receive their living from the gospel*</u> (1 Corinthians 9:14, *NIV*). To the Galatians, he wrote: *Anyone who receives instruction in the word must share all good things with his instructor* (Galatians 6:6, *NIV*).

HOW MUCH SHOULD WE GIVE?
The final question remains. How much should Christians give? Each Christian ... *should give what he has decided in his own heart to give, not reluctantly or under compulsion,*

for God loves a cheerful giver (2 Corinthians 9:7, *NIV*). No set amount or percentage of income is dictated. Rather, ... *if the willingness is there, the gift is acceptable according to what one has, not according to what he does not have* (2 Corinthians 8:12, *NIV*). Does our giving line up with the Scripture?

To summarize, tithing is an attempt to please God based on man's directives. The law of tithing is no different from the other laws the Israelites were given, those that instructed them to kill and sacrifice animals. Jesus was the final sacrifice for sins. God set all the laws, including the Levitical priesthood aside, because they were no longer needed. The laws did what they were supposed to do until Jesus came. The Bible explains their importance in Matthew 22:36-40, in Romans 13:8-10, and again in Galatians 5:14. That is, to love your neighbor as yourself. The Law was given by Moses, but grace and truth was given by Jesus Christ.

CHAPTER ELEVEN

What Should We Do?

In review, Christians should not subject themselves to the Old Testament Law of the Tithe. Instead, they should give according to the following four New Testament guidelines listed below.

Christian giving should be:

- **Proportional to one's income** (1 Corinthians 16:2, 2 Corinthians 8:12)
- **Consistent** (1 Corinthians 16:2)
- **Respectfully** (Mark 12:43-44, 2 Corinthians 8:2-3)
- **Cheerful** (2 Corinthians 9:7)

The Bible is very clear on how the church is commanded to give, thus you should give what God tells you to give. The saints of God should support the church with an open heart and a willing spirit. The saints of God should never feel pressured to give more than they feel comfortable in giving! Should you be indebted to an organization or to Jesus Christ? Many, in the name of Christ Jesus, have given money in vain thinking it was to help win the lost and feed the hungry. Now they have doubts about where the funds went. Was it used to help promote the Gospel, or feed and clothe the needy? Or was it used to promote the selfish? The responsibility of stewardship is in the hands of the recipients. This tax, or tariff, which has been placed on salvation, has left many confused. Yes, salvation is free, but you must pay us to keep it is the attitude implied in many churches. Multitudes of confused Christians could be rescued if the churches would only follow true biblical guidelines concerning giving. God freely gives salvation, but man places organizational assessments on salvation in the form of tithes, which in turn induce grounds for forfeiture of this great gift by legalistic means.

The apostles had numerous opportunities to command the church to pay tithes, but they never did. The apostles never even mentioned the word tithes, except for one occasion which we will discuss later. The apostles only accepted voluntary faith offerings. In the following verses, Paul showed the similarities between the giving of tithes to the priest, and the giving of faith offerings to the preachers of the gospel. The apostle Paul was not saying that preachers should accept tithes. If he wanted to say that, I am sure he would have used the actual word "tithes." He did not use the word "tithes" because that was not what he meant. **The apostles always use the words "giving" or "offering."**

> *Mine answer to them that do examine me is this, Have we not power to eat and to drink? Have we not power to lead about a sister, a wife, as well as other apostles, and as the brethren of the Lord, and Cephas? Or I only and Barnabas, have not we power to forbear working? Who goeth a warfare any time at his own charges? who planteth a vineyard, and eateth not of the fruit thereof? or who feedeth a flock, and eateth not of the milk of the flock? Say I these things as a man? or saith not the*

*law the same also? For it is written in the law of
Moses, Thou shalt not muzzle the mouth of the ox
that treadeth out the corn. Doth God take care for
oxen? Or saith he it altogether for our sakes? For
our sakes, no doubt, this is written: that he that
ploweth should plow in hope; and that he that
thresheth in hope should be partaker of his hope. If
we have sown unto you spiritual things, is it a great
thing if we shall reap your carnal things? If others
be partakers of this power over you, are not we
rather? Nevertheless we have not used this power;
but suffer all things, lest we should hinder the
gospel of Jesus.* **Do ye not know that they which
minister about holy things live of the things of the
temple? and they which wait at the altar are partakers with the altar? Even so hath the Lord
ordained that they which preach the gospel should
live of the gospel** (1 Corinthians 9:3-14, *KJ21*).

Paul was saying that the old covenant servants of God
were receiving according to the old covenant system of giving. The new covenant servants of God receive according to
the new covenant system of giving.

The only Apostolic reference to the word tithes is in
Hebrews 7. The writer is not commanding the new covenant
church to pay tithes. He is saying tithes are under the Law.
And verily they that are of **the sons of Levi, who receive
the office of the priesthood, have a commandment to
take tithes of the people according to the law,** that is, of
their brethren, though they come out of the loins of
Abraham. This entire chapter is about the need of another
priesthood, not another tithe!

WHAT DOES YOUR CHURCH TEACH?
One must really stretch a point to say that Hebrews 7

directs Christian leaders to receive tithes as Melchizedek did, or anyone else for that matter. If Christian leaders want to continue to receive tithes then they should obey the tithing rules laid down in the Law. That is they should skip collecting tithes on the 3rd, 6th, and 7th year. They should ensure that the tithe is eaten in the church, or given to the needy and obey all the regulations associated with tithes. Unfortunately, many so-called Christian leaders play on words to justify a man-made decree of tithing to place judgment and guilt on the unsuspecting believer.

"New covenant teachings are overlooked for old covenant practices, thus limiting both Christian responsibility and freedom due to the church's regulated rules for giving. Christians traditionally give monetary tithes and offerings to the local church. As a result of the rules and obligations of monetary tithing placed upon Christians, some find that they are in the unfortunate position of not being able to fulfill their desire to support those in need. Tithing is not a New Testament principle. We determine this by looking into both the Old and New Testaments. In the New Testament, all references to tithing are either referring to the law or to the practice of Old Testament believers. (See Matthew 23:23, Luke 11:37-44, and Hebrews 7). In the Hebrews 7 reference, the insufficiency of the law is contrasted with New Testament grace. In the Old Testament, the references to tithing were given under the law, which does not apply in the church age." (Andy Neckar)

The apostles could have easily commanded the saints to pay tithes in Acts Chapter 15. They did not record any command to pay tithes. Tithes may have been considered a burden. **I am not saying you should not give to the church! God forbid. What I am saying is that the proper way to give is with faith offerings. The saints of God should give consistently.**

Christians should sit down and consider what he or she

can give on a regular basis. They should also be talking to God about His special desires for others. True friends should be open and honest with each other about their needs, hopes, and dreams. He wants more than friendship with us; He wants a covenant relationship where He can tell us whom to support. The reason He reveals these needs to us is so that we can participate in His plan of fulfilling those hopes, dreams, and desires of His children. When God reveals a special need to us, we should meet that need with joy and praise, and be happy that God found us to be a vessel worthy to be used by Him!

What if an individual or family wanted to voluntarily give 10%? That is fine as long as they understand that the offering is not a tithe. There is nothing evil about giving 10%, but there is something wrong when false teaching is considered the norm. Christians need to study the Scriptures to learn the truth about giving.

None of the following Christian history books, including histories by Henry Chadwick, Foakes Jackson, J.N.D. Kelly, Hans Lietzmann, Andrew Miller, A.H. Newman, or Jaroslav Pelikan have anything to say about tithing in the early church. *The Encyclopedia of Early Christianity* has no entry for the subject. Alan Richardson's *Introduction to the New Testament* has nothing to say on the subject; neither does R.E. Brown's *Introduction to the New Testament*. In research for this study I was amazed to learn that a large percentage of educated Christians understood that tithing was not for New Testaments Christians. Most of them were giving more than 10 % of their incomes for the work of the Lord. They did not call their giving tithing!

In checking the *Ante-* and *Post-Nicene Fathers* (from Clement to beyond Augustine), there is no indication that the early church endorsed any form of tithing. One can trace the quick abrogation of Sabbath observance for Sunday, but there is no clear indication of tithing. I did find the following information on a Catholic Church web page titled New Advent Catholic Encyclopedia. The following article indicates that the Catholic Church reinvented the Law of Tithing just to get more money in their purse.

THE CATHOLIC CHURCH RE-INSTITUTED TITHING FOR CHRISTIANS

In the Christian Church, as those who serve the altar should live by the altar (1 Corinthians 9:13), provision of some kind had necessarily to be made for the sacred ministers. **In the beginning this was supplied by the spontaneous offerings of the faithful.** *In the course of time, however, as the Church expanded and various institutions arose,* **it became necessary to make laws that would ensure the proper and permanent support of the clergy.** *The payment of tithes was adopted* **from the Old Law,** *and early writers speak of it as a divine ordinance and an obligation of conscience. The earliest positive legislation on the subject seems to be contained in the letter of the bishops assembled at Tours in 567 and the cannons of the Council of Macon in 585. In course of time, we find the payment of tithes made obligatory by ecclesiastical enactments in all the countries of Christianity. The Church looked on this payment as "of divine law, since tithes were instituted not by man but by the Lord Himself" (C. 14, X de decim. III, 30). As regards the civil power, the Christian Roman emperors granted the right to churches of retaining a portion of the produce of certain lands, but the earliest instance of the enforcement of the payment of ecclesiastical tithes by civil law is to be found in the capitularies of Charlemagne, at the end of the eighth century. English law very early recognized the tithe, as in the reigns of Athelstan, Edgar, and Canute before the Norman Conquest. In English statute law proper, however, the first mention of tithes is to be found in the Statute of Westminister of 1285. Tithes are of three kinds: predial, or* *that derived from the annual crops; mixed, or what arises from things nourished by the land, as cattle, milk, cheese, wool; and personal or the result of industry or occupation. Predial tithes were generally called great tithes, and mixed and personal tithes, small tithes. Natural substances having no annual increase are not tithable, nor are wild animals. When property is inherited or donated, it is not subject to the law of tithes, but its natural increase is. There are many exempted from the paying of tithes: spiritual corporations, the owners of uncultivated lands, those who have acquired lawful prescription, or have obtained a legal renunciation, or received a privilege from the pope.*

At first, the tithe was payable to the bishop, but later the right passed by common law to parish priests. <u>Abuses soon crept in.</u> The right to receive tithes was granted to princes and nobles, even hereditarily, by ecclesiastics in return for protection or eminent services, and this species of impropriation became so intolerable that the Third Council of Lateran (1179) decreed that no alienation of tithes to laymen was permissible without the consent of the pope. In the time of Gregory VIII, a so-called Saladin tithe was instituted, which was payable by all who did not take part personally in the crusade to recover the Holy Land. At the present time, in most countries where some species of tithes still exist, as in England (for the Established Church), in Austria, and Germany, the payment has been changed into a rent-charge. In English-speaking countries generally, as for as Catholics are concerned, the clergy receive no tithes. As a consequence, other means have had to be adopted to support the clergy and maintain the ecclesiastical institutions (see Church Maintenance), and to substitute other equivalent payments in lieu of tithes. Soglia (Institut, Canon, II, 12) says "<u>The law of tithes</u> can never be abrogated by prescription or custom, if the ministers of the Church have no suitable and sufficient provision from other sources; because then the nat-

ural and divine law, which can neither be abrogated nor anti-
quated, commands that the tithe be paid." It is to be noted
that the custom of paying sacred tithes was not peculiar to
the Israelites, but common to all ancient peoples. In Lydia a
tithe of cattle was offered to the gods; the Arabians paid a
tithe of incense to the god Sabis; and the Carthaginians
brought tithes to Melkarth, the god of Tyre. The explanation
of why the tenth part should have been chosen among so
many different peoples is said to be (apart from a common
primitive revelation) that mystical signification of the number ten, viz., that it signifies totality, for it contains all the
numbers that make up the numerical system, and indeed all
imaginable series of numbers, and so it represents all kinds
of property, which is a gift of God. All species of property
were consequently reckoned in decades, and by consecrating
one of these parts to God, the proprietor recognized the
Source of his goods. However, the payment of tithes was also
a civil custom. They were payable to the Hebrew kings and to
the rulers of Babylon, and they are mentioned among the
Persians, Greeks, Romans, and later the Mohammedans.

Ferraris, Bibliotheca canonica, III (Rome 1886), s.v.,
Decimae; Addis and Arnold, The Catholic Dictionary (6th
ed., New York, 1889), s.v.; Selden, History of Tithes (London,
1618); Spelmen, Of Tythes (London, 1723).

The Catholic Church created the cannon law of tithing as
shown above. It states that the tithing law was adopted from
the old law at the council of Macon 585 A.D. They indicate
that in the beginning they used spontaneous offerings of the
faithful. Then obligatory tithing by ecclesiastical enactments was put into force. As noted above many were exempt
from paying tithes. Abuse of the tithe soon crept in and the
system had to be modified again. It appears that many
protestant organizations preserved this man-made law. In
fact many protestant groups are still under this law today. It
is also interesting to note that neither the Catholic Church,

nor the Jewish religion no longer requires tithing from their members. So why do many protestant churches still teach this lucrative law? The word lucrative could be the answer!

CHAPTER TWELVE

Implications Today

In this book, I have set out to show the following:

1. It was common practice among Gentile nations to pay tithes to their gods.
2. The argument, which claims the universality of the tithing law throughout the Old Testament is unsupportable.
3. The true nature of the Levitical tithe is as follows:
   a. Not all of Israelite society was subject to the agricultural tithes.
   b. Only farmers tithed. Certain professions gave gifts. There was no tithing law for others (fisherman, metal workers, or tent makers) to tithe. Tithes were always agriculture products.
   c. Only a portion of the people's tithes went to the Levites.
   d. The Levites did not have automatic claim to 100% of the people's tithe/offerings.
   e. The tithe was but one segment of the offertory system of ancient Israel.
   f. The tithe benefited the whole of Israelite society.
4. The New Testament Church or its founder (Jesus Christ)

neither collected nor imposed tithes:

   a. Jesus was not influenced by considerations of an ongoing tithing system.

   b. The early church and its work was financed by freewill offerings.

   c. The apostle Paul, who wrote two-thirds of the New Testament made absolutely no claims to any tithes.

5. There is no scriptural validity to support the claims that Christians today are bound by a tithing regime:

   a. The standard for us today is to give bountifully from a cheerful and informed willing heart as God directs us.

   b. There is no reference in the Old Testament or the New Testament stating that the priest, or pastor was to receive the entire tithe.

Carefully consider the following points:

- We need to be fearful of tampering with the Word of God in an attempt to regulate it to our own human ideas, such as presuming to resurrect, legitimize and enshrine a biblical law, a tithing regime long since discarded, and in the process imposing upon God's people today additional financial burdens never intended by God! The church, if it is to reach the world, must learn to live by every Word of God.

- Christians should not prop up an equally unscriptural church government belief based upon the ideas of men rather than the Word of God.

- The testimony of the apostolic church and the teaching of the Scriptures, as illustrated most profusely by the actions and words of the apostle Paul, is that a ministry receives its livelihood from the toil and labor of its Christian brothers and sisters.

- The first century church "turned the world upside-down" (Acts 17:6) with the preaching of the Gospel, which was freely-received and freely-given (Matthew 10:8). They accomplished this without the need to resort to the peddling, or taxing the Word of God (2 Corinthians 2:17). They accomplished this feat by laying no claims to a Levitical tithe, agricultural or otherwise.

- The Holy Spirit is the power and foundation of all the servants of God.

- By contrast, the hierarchical "churches" today seem powerless by ignoring the biblical method of funding the New Testament church established by Jesus and the apostles. They instead, impose upon their adherents an Old Testament *Levitical* Law.

- The words of Jesus will ring loudly against those who collect tithes. *Every plant which My heavenly Father has not planted will be uprooted. Let them alone. They are blind leaders of the blind. And if the blind leads the blind, both will fall into a ditch* (Matthew 15:13-14, *NKJV*).

- If Christians keep the tithing law, and they do not keep the seventh day Sabbath, or circumcision law, (all were instituted BEFORE the law) then they are guilty of breaking all of the law (James 2:10).

What are we going to do about the error that we have been taught for so many years? I am thankful to God for revealing His truth to me. It is now my responsibility to pass it on to others.

God's Guarantees for Giving

MORE REASONS TO GIVE

Although I have said it before, at the risk of being redundant, I am restating that I am not against giving to Christian needs and programs. As a matter of fact, I support many different endevors and encourage others to do so. America is a very blessed nation. We Americans, of all people, should be generous, not only as a nation but also individually. Prosperity should not be used to pad a lavish lifestyle. I believe the purpose of prosperity (being blessed) is to in turn be a blessing to others, especially to those who lack basic necessities.

How many times have you heard the statement in 2 Corinthians 9:7, *For God loves a cheerful giver,* used for raising money for some project which does not help the poor? I say again that there are many more commands, promises, and guarantees given in the Bible for people who give to the poor, than on any other form of giving. At least a portion of the tithe, as directed by God to His people in the Old Testament, was always supposed to be set aside for the poor. Please do not forget the needy. The poor have a tender spot in God's heart. There are many pages of similar commands. I have only listed a few below. There is no need to write a commentary on each verse because each one is self-explanatory.

- *The man with two tunics should share with him who has none, and the one who has food should do the same* (Luke 3:11, *NIV*).
- *Suppose a brother or sister is without clothes and daily food. If one of you says to him, "Go, I wish you well; keep warm and well fed," <u>but does nothing about his physical needs, what good is it?</u>* (James 2:15-16, *NIV*).
- *But <u>when you give to the needy,</u> do not let your left hand know what your right hand is doing, so that your giving may be in secret. Then your Father, who sees what is done in secret, will*

reward you (Matthew 6:3-4, *NIV*).

- *All they asked was that we should continue to remember the poor, the very thing I was eager to do* (Galatians 2:10, *NIV*).
- *Command them to do good, to be rich in good deeds, and to be generous and willing to share* (1 Timothy 6:18, *NIV*).
- *And do not forget to do good and to share with others, for with such sacrifices God is pleased* (Hebrews 13:16, *NIV*).
- *Religion that God our Father accepts as pure and faultless is this: to look after orphans and widows in their distress and to keep oneself from being polluted by the world* (James 1:27, *NIV*).
- *If anyone has material possessions and sees his brother in need but has no pity on him, how can the love of God be in him? Dear children, let us not love with words or tongue but with actions and in truth. This then is how we know that we belong to the truth, and how we set our hearts at rest in his presence* (1 John 3:17-19, *NIV*).
- *If I speak in the tongues of men and of angels, but have not love, I am only a resounding gong or a clanging cymbal* (1 Corinthians 13:1, *NIV*).
- *This is the first and greatest commandment. And the second is like it: Love your neighbor as yourself* (Matthew 22:38-39, *NIV*).
- *The entire law is summed up in a single command: Love your neighbor as yourself* (Galatians 5:14, *NIV*).
- *But he wanted to justify himself, so he asked Jesus, "And who is my neighbor?" In reply Jesus said: "A man was going down from Jerusalem to Jericho, when he fell into the hands of robbers. They stripped him of his clothes, beat him and*

went away, leaving him half dead. A <u>priest</u> happened to be going down the same road, and when he saw the man, he passed by on the other side. So too, a <u>Levite</u>, when he came to the place and saw him, passed by on the other side. But a <u>Samaritan</u>, as he traveled, came where the man was; and when he saw him, he took pity on him. He went to him and bandaged his wounds, pouring on oil and wine. Then he put the man on his own donkey, took him to an inn and took care of him. The next day he took out two silver coins and gave them to the innkeeper. 'Look after him,' he said, 'and when I return, <u>I will reimburse you for any extra expense you may have.</u>' Which of these three do you think was a <u>neighbor</u> to the man who fell into the hands of robbers?" The expert in the law replied, "The one who had mercy on him." Jesus told him, "Go and do likewise." (Luke 10:29-39, *NIV*).

The story Jesus told of the Good Samaritan to indicate what the basic Christian attitude and performance should be. This Samaritan was "good for nothing" and he did his good deed expecting nothing in return. The priest and the Levite overlooked one of the greatest commands that our Lord ever gave. Are modern day priests and pastors overlooking the command of our Lord on helping the poor?

How many times have you heard the above scriptures preached with as much fervor as the preaching of tithing (seldom, if ever I'm sure)? Giving to the poor works because it is the heart beat of a giving God.

I know of numerous individuals who became wealthy because they gave to the needy. Many churches have exploded in growth and financial security because they also gave to those in need. One well-known minister said, "The

Lord told me several years ago to give 10% of my annual income to the poor and needy." He said, "When I obeyed that command my organization grew by leaps and bounds." This man of God is now known worldwide and he will tell you the reason for his success is because he gave to the deprived. He has a huge church, Lear Jets and many acres of land. A geologist told me that two gas wells are producing $200,000 per month on land owned by this "Good Samaritan." Yet, the success of his ministry and personal financial position is not his focus. Saving souls, supporting missionaries who are reaching the ends of the world with the gospel, and seeking more opportunities to give to the poor is his focus. That is why he is flourishing. Many other churches and individuals can give this same testimony.

What is your church doing to help the needy? Do they have a plan to reach out to the poor? Do they care? I suggest that you obtain a copy of your churches financial statement and find out for yourself what percentage of the tithing income goes to the poor. You might be surprised!

CHAPTER THIRTEEN

The Law Clashes With The Holy Spirit

Everything in the New Testament functions according to the Spirit. Our connection to God is a spiritual one. We are not connected to Him by obeying the Law as were the Children of Israel. God wants us to walk in the Spirit (Galatians 5:16), to be led by the Spirit (Romans 8:14), and to make our bodies a spiritual sacrifice (Romans 12:1-3). Everything is by the Spirit. Why would our giving not be by the Spirit? It does not make sense. Requiring people to give under the Law blocks the Holy Spirit's leadership and inspiration for giving. The Holy Spirit is able to not only lead us in our moral, ethical, and spiritual obligations to God and our fellow man, He is able to lead us in our giving. Let me use an example.

LAW OR GRACE?

Just as I started writing this book, I was hit with a big lawsuit that was the result of the American legal system. In our country, anyone can sue anyone anytime for anything. No one needs to have a valid reason. A crooked businessman plus a dishonest lawyer equals a lawsuit in the good old

USA! The devil has many of these types of individuals on his staff. It seems their job description is to aggravate honest hardworking people and unfortunately, our courts are jammed with hundreds of thousands of frivolous lawsuits. The story starts with the day an elderly gentleman contacted me about purchasing some property that I owned. He said that he wanted to use the property to house battered women and the homeless. This got my attention. Battered women and the homeless are worthy causes in my opinion. After review of the property he said he would buy it for $400,000. We signed a contract, but he did not come up with any earnest money. I said, "Sir, we need earnest money to make the contract binding." He refused to put up one cent. He kept assuring me by saying, "I am good for my word. I will have the money in 30 days." Thirty days passed and sure enough he did not close on the property. He asked for two more weeks to get the money. I gave him two more weeks and again he did not come up with the money. It was becoming very obvious that he did not have the money necessary for this purchase.

At the end of the second extension I told him that the deal was off since he would not put up any earnest money. He said, "You will sell me the property or I will sue you and prevent you from selling it to anyone else." Unfortunately, he came through on his threat. In a few days I received a summons from the County Sheriff's Department to appear in court for a $600,000 lawsuit.

I incurred attorney fees of over $12,000 in defending myself to prove my innocence. Finally, the old fellow dropped the lawsuit after he realized that I would not agree to a big settlement just to resolve the case.

The old devil tried to beat me up about this lawsuit. I just kept reminding the Lord that since everything I have belongs to Him; it was His lawsuit. I am only a steward of what He allows me to own. Although the entire process was aggravating, time consuming, and expensive, I had peace from beginning to end. I did exactly what Jesus said to do about such cases. *Bless those who curse you, pray for those who mistreat you* (Luke 6:28, *NIV*). I prayed for the old man's soul many times. And I continued to give to the Lord's work. I was not about to let this trivial lawsuit come between the Lord and me.

Here is the rest of the story. Remember that the old fellow had offered me $400,000 for the property (although I would have gladly taken $200,000). While the litigation was in process another individual gave me a backup contract, with earnest money, for $400,000. As soon as the legal proceedings were over the second contract was valid for the full amount. I said, "Thank you, devil, for increasing the sales price of the property from $200,000 to $400,000." My little $12,000 bill for attorney fees was returned to me many times over. Of course, the Lord had it all under control the whole time.

YOUR PROBLEMS ARE GOD'S OPPORTUNITY

It is so wonderful to let God work out your problems! He will protect your interests if you adhere to His written guarantees. I discovered a long time ago that God is the best business partner to have. I learned this unforgettable lesson when a man I'll call John cheated others and myself out of thousands of dollars. He caused my family agony for years.

While in the midst of the turmoil created by John, I said to myself late one night, "I wish John was in hell for all the trouble he has caused me." I will never say that again! About 2:00 A.M. I had a dream about John. He was in hell. His flesh was burning. He was screaming, and pleading with me to get him out of there. Needless to say I got up out of bed and began praying for John that very moment. In just a few days he called me early one morning weeping and said, "Ron, please forgive me for all that I have done to you, I am so sorry." Of course I was eager to forgive him. Ever since then my attitude has changed regarding people who try to cheat me. Never again would I want even my worst enemy to be in hell. The Lord says, *Love your enemies and pray for those who persecute you, that you may be sons of your Father in heaven* (Matthew 5:44-45, *NIV*).

THE DANGER OF THE WORD "TITHE" FOR CHRISTIANS!

I make the following observations humbly and only after years of study, hours of prayer, self-examination, and many conversations with my fellow Christians friends. To be honest, I was shocked at what I learned about tithing in the New Testament.

One might say, "What difference does it make that I call my giving tithes? When I was tithing, all the money was going to the Lord." I have heard many similar statements from those who tithe.

Deception has never been a part of the plan of God. Jesus said that knowing and doing the truth sets men free (John 8:32). Since tithing is not a requirement for Christians, if it is taught or tolerated then Christians are believing a lie. This deception has spread to many Christian organizations over the years. It is passed along to the members as fact. The leadership and the members follow this man-made law as if it were straight out of the New Testament. It is not. If the Law is still in effect then Jesus died in vain (Galatians 2:21).

THE FIX

One should never present a problem without a means or recommendation of how to solve the predicament. The tithing dilemma may seem impossible to resolve because it is such a universal formula for Christian economy. Many Christian leaders will agree that the word tithing is the "monetary catalyst" that compels members to give. Why not teach the biblical way of giving and yield biblical results? We read in this book that the First Church grew beyond measure by receiving support from the new Christians. These churches did not require tithes, nor did they accept them.

Tithing can actually be very restrictive. The term "tithe" can water down the real meaning of giving and thereby forfeit expected blessings. Please insure that you are giving in accordance with the Word of God rather than the word of man. When man and his ways have replaced God and His ways, (the Word), then man and his system become like a god.

CHRISTIAN LEADERSHIP

David and his leaders collected over $4 billion to build a temple. How was it done? The answer is found in 1 Chronicles 29:1-18. The following is a summary of his pledge program.

- David gave to the cause *first*, providing an example for the people to follow. He did not expect the people to do what he did not do.
- He asked for volunteers, willing contributors. Notice that he did not coerce the people to give.
- His leaders responded first, before the people did. I want to comment on this point before going on. David did not have to coerce the leaders to give. David's integrity, compassion, and purity of intent spoke for themselves. His leaders under him had reason to be wholeheartedly committed to the work at hand. David was a worthy leader, worthy of support. The people responded willingly, following the example set by David and his leaders.
- There was so much cooperation that David had to ask them to stop giving!

The same method of giving was used in the New Testament to support the work of the Lord. I believe the lesson we can learn from David's building project is that when financial support is given God's way, the Holy Spirit and God's wonderful people make a good partnership. More than enough money will be collected to do the job. On the other hand, if church leaders believe they must coerce the people by preaching the Law instead of grace, then neither the Holy Spirit nor the people will operate at full potential.

Tithing can also be restrictive for the church. Statistics show that less than 20% of Americans tithe. If they were taught that each should "give as he purposes in his heart," then participation in financial support might increase and close in the gap. More would be willing to give if they could give "according to their income" and were free to follow the Holy Spirit.

"TEN REASONS WHY I TITHE" TRACT

The above title, TEN REASON WHY I TITHE, is taken from a tract that is distributed by a large denomination to all its churches for justification of tithing. They use the indicated scriptures to try to prove that tithing is valid for New Testament Churches. I will list the verse they use and paraphrase their reasons to tithe. You can be the judge of their intent.

- To honor the Creator. *Render ... unto God the things that are God's* (Matthew 22:21). This vague attempt to declare that the above verse is a command to tithe is ridiculous to say the least.
- To acknowledge my heritage. *And if ye be Christ's then are ye Abraham's seed, and heirs according to the promise* (Galatians 3:29). They say that Abraham was the first tithe payer and since we are his spiritual seeds we are obligated

164

to pay tithes. It is recorded in the Bible and I discussed in this book that Abram only paid tithes one time. Would this organization be willing for their members to pay tithes only once? Father Abraham had concubines as we read in Genesis 25. Does the above logic mean that we should have concubines as well?

- To fulfill the Covenant. *For if that which is done away was glorious, much more that which remaineth is glorious* (II Corinthians 3:11). Using this beautiful verse to prove tithing is a feeble attempt to control the uninformed.

- To show my Love. *Many waters cannot quence love* (Song of Solomon 8:7). They say in their tract, "Someone should print a bumper sticker that says, 'If you love Jesus, pay you tithes!'" The subject here is love, not tithing, grace, not Law! The following beautiful statement is from the Internet, Author Unknown. "The old covenant required simple percentages. Everyone knew how much was required. The new covenant has no set percentages. Instead, it requires more soul-searching, more training for the conscience, more selfless love for others, more faith, more voluntary sacrifice and less compulsion. It tests our values, what we treasure most, and where our hearts are."

- To fulfill an obligation. *Ye pay tithe …: these ought ye to have done, and not to leave the other undone* (Matthew 23:23). As I recorded in this book Jesus scolded these religious leaders, who were still under the law, because they had neglected the more important matters of law which He said was justice, mercy, and faithfulness. This statement by Jesus was said before the New Testament Church began.

- To escape condemnation. *Will a man rob God? Yet ye have robbed me ... in tithes and offerings* (Malachi 3:8). Again this is the fear factor that they try to place on their members who question paying tithes. As recorded in Malachi God was speaking to the priest who were robbing Him not to the people.

- To spread the Gospel. *So hath the Lord ordained that they which preach the gospel should live of the gospel* (I Corinthians 9:14). This is a very true statement, but their living does not come from tithes. As I explained in this book, Paul and all other New Testament preachers obtained their funds from cheerful givers. Tithing was never the source of their income.

- To avoid a curse. *Ye are cursed with a curse: for ye have robbed me* (Malachi 3:9). The fear factor is used again by those who teach the tithing curse from the Old Testament. I challenge you to read all of Malachi and see who is doing the robbing!

- To enjoy God's blessings. *Bring ye all the tithes into the storehouse ... and prove me now herewith, saith the Lord of hosts, if I will not open you the windows of heaven, and pour you out a blessing, that there shall not be room enough to receive it* (Malachi 3:10). The church was never spoken of as a storehouse for the Lord's goods. Churches were not intended to store livestock and crops as I stated earlier in this book. Old Testament tithing was always agriculture products and was never money. This is a very weak attempt to plant false promises in the heart and mind of the sincere contributor.

- To be consistent. *Be thou an example of the believers* (I Timothy 4:12). If they want their members to be consistent they should teach the New Testament command for giving. *Each man should give what he has decided in his heart to give, not reluctantly or under compulsion, for God loves a cheerful giver* (II Corinthians 9:6, *NIV*).

The above ten reasons for New Testament Christians to tithe have no legitimate biblical basis at all. It is hard for me to believe that honest, spirit filled, and somewhat educated pastors can truthfully teach these tithing commands to their sincere members. The Lord said, *"... The prophets <u>prophesy lies, the priest rule by their own authority</u>, and <u>my people love it this way</u>. But what will you do in the end"* (Jeremiah 5:31, *NIV*)?

CHAPTER FOURTEEN

Conclusions

My friends and fellow Christians, after all the evidence that has been submitted it is inconceivable to me that anyone could believe tithing has any relevance in the New Testament church. Although there are a lot of places where tithing could be discussed, there is no command in the New Testament stating that Christians are required to tithe. Tithing as such has no bearing on the New Testament church at all.

BE GENTLE WITH THIS TRUTH

Hopefully, after reading all the related scriptures in this book you can now understand that the command of tithes is not part of the New Testament Church. Please do not attack your pastor with all this truth at once. Talk with him about this matter in private. Do not *demand* changes. Do not organize others to take over the church. Give your spiritual leaders a copy of this book and let them better understand what the Bible teaches about giving. In all probability this information will be a threat to their financial security. It should not be intimidating if they understand the Bible. But many Christian leaders are not very well versed in this area. Give your pastor time to absorb God's information on this subject. But, more importantly, pray for him. Never use your newfound knowledge to split the church, or to start rumors about the financial department of the church.

My fellow Christians, if you want to be blessed for your faithful giving, please obey the New Testament commands so that the guarantees will flow into your purse. Ensure that part of your giving helps the needy as the Lord commands in Matthew Chapter 25. **Jesus said you would burn if you do not feed the hungry!** Check this out for yourself. Your earthly financial statement will increase, and your eternal financial statement will increase as well if you comply with the Lord's commands. We should allow the Spirit to lead us to give according to our means. The world would then finally get a glimpse of true Christianity and the kingdom of God expanding on the earth.

INCREASE YOUR GIVING

This study *God's Guarantees for Giving* should encourage you to increase your giving. Our Savior, who has made many positive promises, is eager to bless you if you obey His commands. Jesus said, *Give, and it will be given unto you. A good measure, pressed down, shaken together and running over, will be poured into your lap. For with the measure you use, it will be measured to you* (Luke 6:38, *NIV*).

I love the Church. The Body of Christ is the representation of Christ on the earth. We are His hands and feet. We also hold His wallet. The local church is God's instrument of presenting the gospel to the world. I would never willingly do anything or say anything to harm the church or its financial system. However, I do love the church enough to challenge the entire Christian financial system to get us back on track with the Lord's way of giving. And by accomplishing this I believe the churches will expand in size. Like the church of the first century, we could "turn the world upside down!"

EXAMPLES OF GIVING

The remaining portion of this chapter lists some of the ministries that I support in my plan to obey the New Testament commands of generosity. Although I would encourage anyone to support the ministries listed below, I only use the following as examples. I am thankful the Lord has allowed me to join His cause through these ministries. I suggest that you pray about this subject, and I assure you that the Lord will lead you in wisdom and direction. He will let you know how much you should give, when you should give and to whom you should give. He loves a cheerful giver. Zaccheus understood giving when he was saved. He said that he gave half of his goods to the poor. Fifty percent is not a tithe. It is a gift!

Please note that I have a variety of worthy groups that I give too. In the business world this mixture of resources is called "asset allocation." With this type of giving, or investing in God's kingdom, your eternal financial statement is spread around all over the world. For example, on a given day souls may cost less to win in Russia than in America. Of course you want to get the maximum amount of souls for your investment. Some soul investments are like growth stock, some are like value stock, and some are safe and secure as bonds. No matter what you pick, your assets are recorded, not on "Wall Street," but on "Heavenly Way." The retirement is out of this world!

DAILY BREAD MINISTRY

This ministry in Fort Worth, TX, feeds and supplies clothing to hundreds of homeless several times a week. They have a wonderful church service for these destitute souls before feeding them. Many have been saved through their effort and have been elevated into good paying jobs. In addition to reaching their city, Daily Bread has grown so large that it now supplies needed items to more than one hundred and fifty missions worldwide. The reason I support Daily

Bread is because in prayer quite some time ago, I asked the Lord whom should I help in obeying Matthew 25. I heard the name Roy Gray amplified loud and clear in my mind! I had not thought of Roy, the founder and director of Daily Bread, in months. Needless to say, Daily Bread received a check from me that week.

Roy told me about a well-dressed man who came by his office recently and asked if there was anything that the ministry needed. Roy, who works on faith, said that they could use a new tent for their services. The man inquired about the cost and Roy told him that it would be $9,250. The man pulled out his checkbook and wrote the ministry a check for $9,250. Then he told Roy, "I was homeless a few years ago and your ministry fed me. The Lord has restored my profession and I am doing very well spiritually and financially. I am thankful for what you did for me and I want to help others who are homeless." Roy told me, "You see they are not all bums." It is recorded, *Then the King will say to those on his right, "Come, you who are blessed by my Father; take your inheritance, ... For I was hungry and you gave me something to eat, I was thirsty and you gave me something to drink, I was a stranger and you invited me in, I needed clothes and you clothed me..."* (Matthew 25:35-36, *NIV*).

DR. JAMES DOBSON WITH
FOCUS ON THE FAMILY

I support this ministry because Dr. Dobson is the mouthpiece for Christians nationwide. Focus on the Family attacks the anti-Christian issues that emerge from the pits of hell. They are on the forefront when proposed laws are designed to undermine our nation's Christian heritage. It is unfortunate that many Christian organizations do not want to leave the security of their four walls to be heard on international issues that affect our religious future. Thank God for men like Dr. James Dobson and others who attack and expose those who are trying to destroy our freedom of religion. *The entire law is summed up in a single command: Love your neighbor as yourself* (Galatians 5:14, NIV).

JAMES ROBISON WITH LIFE OUTREACH

I have visited the offices of this fine ministry and have seen firsthand that they do, in fact, feed thousands of hungry children around the world. This network of Christian professionals spends endless hours supplying food to starving children in many countries. Life Outreach is worthy. Jesus said, ... *When you give a banquet, invite the poor, the crippled, the lame, the blind, and you will be blessed. Although they cannot repay you, you will be repaid at the resurrection of the righteous* (Luke 14:12-14, NIV).

RUSSIA AND OTHER FOREIGN COUNTRIES

For years, as a Navy Fighter Pilot, I was trained to destroy the Communist. Now, instead of delivering bombs, we are delivering Bibles. Instead of launching missiles, we have launched a mission to introduce these wonderful souls to Jesus. For years we have heard the slogan, "I had rather be dead than Red." The Lord removed the "Wall" and gave us a golden opportunity to reach those hungry souls. One of the highlights of my life was teaching in a Russian Bible School in St. Petersburg, Russia and also teaching Bible Studies in Romania. I have a special place in my heart for those whom I was once trained to kill. This is a fantastic way to increase our eternal financial statement and receive blessings in the here and now. *Cornelius stared at him in fear. "What is it, Lord?" he asked. The angel answered, "Your prayers and gifts to the poor have come up as a memorial offering before God"* (Acts 10:4, NIV).

JESUS WEPT MINISTRY

A few years ago Sister Vicki Robinson gave me the

opportunity to adopt (by monthly support) six children in India. We have received pictures of the three boys and three girls and have corresponded with them. For just a few dollars a month we have made a great difference in the children's future ... and great difference in our eternal future. Thanks, Sister Vicki for the opportunity. The Bible states, *Religion that God our Father accepts as pure is this: to look after the orphans and widows in their distress ...*(James 1:27, *NIV*).

CREATION EVIDENCE MUSEUM

Dr. Carl Baugh, PhD, has proven without a doubt, that evolution is one of the biggest lies that the devil has placed in the minds of mankind. He and a team of scientists use science and the Bible to prove that Almighty God created the universe and all living things therein. He is broadcasting this knowledge around the world to win more souls for our Savior. Thanks, Dr. Baugh for your knowledge and your challenge to the youth of our generation. I am proud to be a part of your team. Paul said, *I urged you when I went into Macedonia, ...that you may command certain men not to teach false doctrine any longer nor to devote themselves to myths and endless genealogies* (I Timothy 1:3, *NKJV*).

APOSTOLIC WORLD CHRISTIAN FELLOWSHIP

Bishop Samuel Smith is the leader of more than one hundred and fifty Christian organizations that have bound together as one to reach the lost world for Jesus. The AWCF has missions active in numerous countries around the world preaching the gospel. They have a very low budget but are able to win more souls per dollar than any other group I know. Jesus said, *Therefore go and make disciples of all nations ... teaching them to obey everything I have commanded you* (Matthew 28:19, *NIV*).

INTERNATIONAL FELLOWSHIP OF
CHRISTIAN BUSINESSMEN

This worldwide organization, under the leadership of Bill Wilkerson, a businessman, is establishing IFCB chapters to reach people in the workplace. In addition, they feed the hungry in many major cities in the USA. IFCB has led many businessmen to the saving knowledge of Jesus Christ. Jesus said, *I tell you, use your worldly wealth to gain friends for yourselves, so that when it is gone, you will be welcomed into eternal dwellings* (Luke 16:9, *NIV*).

BIBLE SCHOOLS

Worthy Bible schools that are teaching the New Testament plan of salvation are another great opportunity to invest into the kingdom of God. These young Christian men and women, who will be our spiritual leaders of tomorrow, need all the financial help and encouragement that we can give them. *Then he opened their minds so they could understand the Scriptures* (Luke 24:47, *NIV*).

CHRISTIAN TELEVISION AND
RADIO BROADCASTERS

There are a few good ones who get the message out to the people. This media is able to penetrate the walls of high-rise apartments, nursing homes, hospitals, prisons and other locations that may be impracticable for others to reach. Thousands in Russia first heard of Jesus via this media. I actually received the Baptism of the Holy Spirit sitting in Pat Robinson's TV studio (700 Club) in Dallas, TX over twenty years ago. Trinity Broadcast Network is telling the world about Jesus. DayStar with Marcus and Joni Lamb are reaching many across the nation. Mike Simons Ministries delivers a very powerful soul saving message. I witnessed Marcs Lamb and Mike Simons writing big checks to help spread the gospel in Russia. Dr. Garth Coonce of Marion, IL has great Christian programs. And there are many more productions and preachers trying to reach souls for our Savior. Jesus said, *Go into all the world and preach the good news to all creation* (Mark 16:15, *NIV*).

HOME CHURCH

By supporting all of the above and many other ministries, the Lord has blessed me financially so that I can still give more than ten percent to my home church. This support is for pastoral salary, building programs, education programs and whatever the church needs. The Bible is clear on the fact that the more you give, the more you get, thereby the more you have to give. Jesus recorded, *Give, and it will be given unto you. A good measure, pressed down, shaken together and running over, will be poured into your lap. For with the measure you use, it will be measured to you* (Luke 6:38, *NIV*).

None of the above giving is considered tithing. There are no commands for tithing in the New Testament as I have explained in this book. Since there are no commands to tithe in the New Testament there are not any guaranteed blessings for tithing. As you have read in this report, the greatest financial insurance available is giving God's way. When you give God's way you do not have to worry if your financial status appears to be headed for disaster. You have the guarantee, as I did, that the Lord will work miracles in your behalf. God's Word is all I need. He will fight my battles, and the bottom line will always be in the green if I obey Him. He honors His Word. No lawyer, judge, banker, nor broker can give you that kind of guarantee.

PASTORS

My pastor friends, please know that I am neither against you nor your income-stream, or by whatever means you have in force for collection. I am against anyone who takes advantage of sincere souls with the outdated law of tithing!

I caution you not to appeal for, nor accept tithes from your members since this doctrine has no New Testament basis. If you must continue collecting tithes, then make sure that it is given in agricultural units (meat or grain, not money), eaten in the storehouse, given to the poor, stranger, fatherless and widows as recorded in the Law. And remember that there was no tithing during the seventh year.

The Bible promises you much greater abundance if you allow your members to give GOD'S WAY. You do not need to fear losing your big tithe payers by telling them the truth. In fact the church's income should increase because of the guarantees God has placed on His methods of giving. I had been a big tithe payer for years. Now I am more excited about giving God's way. I have increased my giving, knowing that I am in line with the apostolic method of charity.

The New Testament instructions provide you a double blessing, as recorded in 1 Timothy, 5:17, *The elders who direct the affairs of the church well are worthy of a double honor, especially those whose work is preaching and teaching (NIV).* And in Galatians 6:6 Paul says, *Anyone who receives instruction in the word must share all good things with his instructor (NIV).* The tithing law did not provide you with that kind of increase. Pastors have it made with the New Testament order for your compensation and you do not need the false pretense of tithing for your salaries. I have always maintained that the pastors, who are preaching truth, should be amongst the highest paid personnel in their cities. Their responsibility demands the pay and they are worthy of it.

Are you going to teach Law, or justified by faith? *For as many as are of the works of the law are under the curse: for it is written, Cursed is every one that continueth not in all things which are written in the book of the law to do them. But that no man is justified by the law in the sight of God, it is evident: for, The just shall live by faith. And the law is not of faith: but, The man that doeth them shall live in them.*

Christ hath redeemed us from the curse of the law, being made a curse for us ... (Galatians 3:10-13).

Many sincere pastors have put the Bible back in the churches as the rulebook to follow on giving. These genuine men of God are taking much verbal abuse from their self-righteous brothers. However, they are man enough and spiritual enough to say, "We are no longer going to take advantage of sincere souls, by teaching commands of man about giving that are not found in the Bible."

This may be hard for you pastors to believe, but I am excited about the possibilities if you change to God's way of giving and receiving. Imagine seeing the positive results which will occur in your church. Your members will be blessed as well. The Word of God guarantees these financial blessings. Prayerfully consider getting back on track with the giving methods used and taught by the first Apostolic Church. Provide an outlet for your members to support the needy at all times. Let them assist in distributing food and clothing to the needy. I feel the exhilaration of the Holy Ghost as I relate these promises written in the New Testament.

CHRISTIANS

My fellow Christians, if you want to be blessed for your faithful giving, please obey the New Testament commands and the guarantees will flow into your purse. Insure that part of your giving helps the needy, as the Lord commands in Matthew Chapter 25. Jesus said <u>you would burn if you do not feed the hungry!</u> Check this out for yourself. Your earthly economic statement will increase, and your eternal wealth will increase as well if you comply with the Lord's commands. We should allow the Spirit to lead us to give according to our means and ability. The world would then finally get a glimpse of true Christianity and the kingdom of God expanding on the earth. This study should encourage you to increase your giving, because of all the positive promises by our Savior who is eager to bless you if you obey His commands.

> *When reading that we should not tithe, do not assume that it means we should stop giving to the Lord or stop supporting the local church. These two concepts are completely unrelated. The local church is a good work and should continue, but through grace, as led by the Holy Spirit, and with the correct priorities in place.* (Extracted from an introduction to the book *Beyond Tithes & Offerings* by Michael L. Webb & Mitchell T. Webb)

According to an article in *Charisma* magazine, August 2001 edition, page 36, *Church giving takes a downward turn. Churches could face a crisis because of changing attitudes about the collection plate. According to researcher George Barna, giving to churches dropped significantly last year. Seventy percent of born-again Christians gave to the church last year, down from 84 percent in 1999. The survey also found that although 32 percent of believers said they tithed, a check of household income found that only 12 percent actually did.* It is my belief that Christians would give more if they knew the Scriptures and the biblical way of giving and receiving. I believe this is so because the Holy Spirit would have more influence on the hearts of the people. Also, God's grace would be more effective in their lives because they would be under grace and not under the Law.

Please review the many guaranteed statements in the New Testament establishing financial blessings for giving God's way. Not once was tithing commanded in the New Testament, therefore there are no blessings for paying such. Giving God's way was commanded. Coupled with the command were either guarantees or judgment. I have related several financial blessings that the Lord sent my way because I obeyed His Word. His Word is the reason we are blessed, not because of any favoritism to me or anyone else.

THE DEVIL IS A LOSER

I only relate the following fact in hopes that it might help someone who may be in a similar situation. "Another business deal has gone bad," I said to my wife. The problem with this company is that I found out too late that the managers were crooks. To make a long story short I was set up by a reprobate. He departed with the money and I was left with a $625,000 note due and payable to a local bank. I had no control of the company and no way to redeem my situation. When I went to court I was not allowed to tell my entire story because of the wretched legal system of this country. I never received one cent of the $625,000. But, the judge placed a binding judgment on me for $650,000. He raised the amount $25,000, I suppose to impress the banks that were supporting him. The judgment was filed in several counties. For eight years I could not borrow one cent. Somehow I knew that the Lord was going to work out my problem, but I did not know how or when. I had faith in my Heavenly Banker. One point that I want to emphasize is that during that period of time I did not reduce one penny on my giving. I told my wife, "Everything we have belongs to the Lord, even the $650,000 judgment. He owns everything and He is my heavenly Father so why should we worry?" No one but my family members knew of this dilemma. Of course I did fret at times but was soon assured by the Word that everything would work out. I was willing to accept whatever the final resolve might be. With interest added each year it did not take long until the judgment grew to more than a million dollars.

The bank that held the judgment was trying to schedule a payment plan for me when they developed serious internal financial problems. They were forced to sell my judgment to another firm for a few cents on the dollar. Of course this new firm notified me that I owed them over one million dollars. We swapped strong letters for a while, and then their letters stopped suddenly. I did a little investigating and found out that they had gone bankrupt. There were some happy Texans praising the Lord at my house. The next big test was to see if the judgments had been taken off my record at the many county courthouses across the state and with the credit bureau. Sure as the Lord lives, all records of the judgment were erased. WOW! That is the kind of God I serve and that is the kind of God you serve. He will fight your battles for you, if you let Him.

I could relate many more financial miracles that the Lord has provided for my family and for others as well. I only hope this first-hand information about my personal giving and receiving will inspire others to give and receive. Remember God's guarantees!

Why are some not blessed for giving? Simply because Bible truth has become unbalanced and exaggerated by many who are teaching false doctrine. This deception has again elevated Law above grace. This deceit, either intentional or by ignorance, has created Christians who do not understand Christianity. As you can tell by the examples listed in this study and from your own personal experiences the repercussions of man-made giving has sent a shockwave through some Christian organizations. I am convinced that this action by man has provided a strong support system that the old devil has used to his advantage to suppress Christianity. There is no need for Satan to eliminate the biblical way in order to cause confusion in giving methods among Christians. Christian leaders have already completed that task in many organizations.

I challenge you, my brothers and sisters, to search God's Word for truth. <u>Listen to God.</u> Ask God to give you courage enough to execute His commands. <u>Listen to God.</u> Then share the love of God and the Word of God, with the children of God. If my words herein have offended you then please forgive me. If God's Word has offended you then repent and start preaching and teaching and giving His way. The challenge is before you, my brothers and sisters, to prayerfully search God's Word for the truth concerning giving. Everyone should be free to give everything, but no one is free to demand anything but love. Give regularly, proportionally, willingly, and knowingly.

SECRET FOR SUCCESS

Many are quick to say, "You make a lot of money because you are a businessman and understand how to start companies and deal with the financial world." Little do they know that I cut logs and loaded lumber to get through college. My family was poor. In fact my entire hometown of 150 souls were poor. None of us had indoor plumbing. Many did not have electricity. There was only one hand cranked telephone in my town. My future did not look too bright from that little country town. So what is my secret for success? I am glad that you asked.

I believe that the Lord blesses those who financially support His causes with business principles and plans. We just need to take advantage of opportunities He brings our way. We must act on the business inspiration that He gives. We all know that He feeds the birds, but he does not put the food in their nest. We must act in faith that our business plan will work. One can seed his success in any legitimate business deal with prayer and proper giving. Then adopt the theory that everything belongs to the Lord, including your business. And by faith and hard work watch your financial statement grow.

For example, a wild thought came to me a few years ago about the possibility of selling Mercedes Benz automobiles to airline employees who were traveling to Europe. I had read that one could purchase a Mercedes through a Mercedes dealer in the states and take delivery of the car in Germany at a substantial discount. Since airline crewmembers were traveling to Europe they could take advantage of the lower price on these fine automobiles. Now the tough part of this thought is the fact that I had never sold a car of any kind. How could I possibly start selling the best car made? Remember what I said above, "Seed your business with prayer and giving." That is all I had. It was enough.

I spoke with a local Mercedes dealer about representing his European Delivery Program to European travelers. To my surprise the dealer liked the plan. Within a few months, and with a lot of hard work, we were the largest selling force for European Delivery of Mercedes in the nation. I was able to hire a lot of church members to help run the business. We also supported more than 25 missionaries from the income of that one company. I give God all the credit for that financial miracle.

No, I am not bragging on myself. I am only telling you that God will bless you with business plans if you will put Him first with your finances. If you will open your wallet for Him, He will open your mind with good business principles and you will be successful.

In *God's Guarantees for Giving* you have read how the Lord:

- Gave me four producing oil wells that produced over $2 million.
- Cancelled a note that I owed that was $1.5 million.
- Cancelled a judgment against me for more than $1 million.
- Gave me prosperous business deals that I could only dream about.
- And many more miracles.

If He will do this for me, He will do it for you, if you only obey his Word. He does not honor me above anyone, but He honors His Word above everything! It is a delight to watch how the Lord blesses His people who obey Him. His guarantees never fail!

If God's guarantees fail then we have the right to question the virgin birth, the resurrection, and the second coming of Jesus!

MY PRAYER

O Lord God, the Creator of the Universe, and all that there is therein,

Your Majesty and Splendor is beyond comprehension of mankind.

The earth is Your footstool; the mountain flees at Your presence.

I am but a crumb in quest of Truth from Your Greatness.

I humbly bow before You, pleading for Your

Will to be accomplished with this book.

Allow Truth to rise above tradition,

let Your Will be known.

Amen!

My people know not the ordinance of the Lord ... Lo, they have rejected the word of the Lord And what wisdom is in them?
(Jeremiah 8: 7-9)

Have I now become your enemy by telling you the truth (Galatians 4:16, *NIV*)?

How to Judge a Healthy, Sound Ministry

It is the responsibility of the individual believer to look into each ministry (including his home church) and make informed, purposeful decisions about whom they will support. To help you know how to judge whether a ministry is healthy, sound, and worthy of your financial generosity, I have included some guidelines.

• The minister who is worthy of support will encourage you to seek the truth for yourself and to be submitted to God. He will not set himself up as the final authority who should not be questioned (like a god). An abusive leader will either overtly or covertly teach you that being loyal/submissive to him is the same as being submissive to God. When this abuse is covert it is more difficult to recognize. This message is subtle. We can see through the smoke screen when the leader is neither demanding nor hinting at submission to him rather than God. He is grace-filled and allows people to be accountable to God. IIe is supportive, as well as truthful. His integrity, the credibility of his life, and the purity of his message will demonstrate the authority, spiritual power, and wisdom with which God has bestowed to him. His message will set people free to serve God; it will not put them in bondage to serving him or to serving the system (the church). The church does provide ministries in which we can serve. However, the difference between a healthy ministry and an abusive ministry, is that a healthy minister does not have to coerce his members to serve. He provides the platform, and the people volunteer out of love and the recognition of a need. They do not respond out of manipulation or guilt. The Scripture says that pastors are to, *Be shepherds of God's flock that is under your care, serving as overseers—not because you must, but because you are willing, as God wants you to be; not greedy for money, but eager to serve; not lording it over those entrusted to you, but being examples to the flock. And when the Chief Shepherd appears, you will receive the crown of glory that will never fade away* (1 Peter 5:2-4, *NIV*).

• A minister worthy of your support will not be preoccupied with your performance. He will truly understand salvation and apply its truth to his own life so that he can teach the truth to others. Salvation comes by faith through grace, provided by the blood Jesus shed for our sins. Salvation does not come through obeying the law. Neither does sanctification come through obeying the law, but through grace and faith in the blood of Jesus and by being led and guided by the Holy Spirit. A minister worthy of your support will not be performance-based in his teaching. He will be grace-based.

• A minister worthy of support will have your best interest at heart. He will not be motivated by his own driven need for profit, power, pleasure, and/or prestige. When Jesus asked Peter if he loved Him and Peter said yes, Jesus said, *Then feed my sheep* (see John 21:16-17). A true minister will feed you the Word of God out of his love for Jesus, out of his desire to glorify God through his ministry, and out of your need for spiritual nourishment. He will not use the Word to serve his own purposes in order to control you.

• A good rule of thumb is to know where the funds are going. If you are going to give then you have a right to know where the money is going. I recommend you request a financial statement which shows how much of the funds are designated for salaries, how much goes to administrative fees, and how much actually goes to help the poor and/or needy. Anyone who becomes offended or gets defensive when you ask for such information has something to hide. Even if their motives are pure, they may lack good stewardship and would certainly want to keep their poor stewardship from being discovered. God will judge us based on our own stewardship, not someone else's. We must take responsibility for finding out where our money is going.

I have visited most of the ministries that I support to ensure that they are authentic stewards of the Lord's money. The ones that I cannot visit I investigate via other means. I suggest you be bold enough to ask sensitive questions. Those who are worthy of your gifts will not be ashamed to answer such questions.

In *The Midas Touch, A Balanced Approach to Biblical Prosperity*, Reverend Kenneth E. Hagin provides some guidelines for giving. I believe they are healthy, rational guidelines and have also included them here.

Believers should look for organizations to support that are productive for the Kingdom of God, ministries that are actively contributing to the preaching of the Gospel and the expansion of the Church. A prospective giver might ask questions such as the following:

• *How many people are being born again and filled with the Spirit through this ministry?*

• *How many people are being established and*

strengthened in the faith through its outreaches?
- *Is multiplication taking place? Are ministers being produced and churches being established?*
- *Is good being accomplished in the world and in the Body of Christ through this ministry?*
- *Is its message one of truth?*
- *Is the ministry a good steward of its finances?*
- *Are the methods used in ministry and in fundraising ethical and wholesome?*
- *Is the ministry (and its ministers) financially accountable?*

There are also some 'red flags' or warning signs to watch for in determining whether a ministry is sound and worthy of support. I would suggest the utmost caution in supporting or being involved with any organization that has the following marks:

- *Exerts pressure to give or encourages impulse giving by saying, 'You must give now!'*
- *Makes suggestions of condemnation and guilt if you don't give.*
- *Uses hype, emotionalism, and spiritual manipulation, such as 'prophesying' dollars out of your pocket.*
- *Makes outlandish promises such as, 'Everyone who gives now will receive a hundredfold return.' or, 'Those who give to this offering will have your debts canceled.'*
- *Does not promote the local church, or projects the idea that theirs is the only ministry worth supporting.*
- *Spends more time and energy raising funds than in doing the work of the ministry.*

- *Builds money appeals around gimmicks and sensationalism.* (p. 203-204, *The Midas Touch, A Balanced Approach to Biblical Prosperity*).

Ultimately, the responsibility is yours. You cannot blindly give money away and expect God to bless you for your giving if He does not place His stamp of approval on the organizations to which you give.

Bibliography

Arterburn, Stephen, *Toxic Faith,* (WalterBrook Press, a division of *Random House, Inc.,*) 1991, 2001.

Bruce, F.F., *New Testament History*; p 142.

Bunyan, John, *Quotes,* 1628-1688.

Charisma & Christian Life magazine, *Letters to the Editor,* December 2001.

Decimea: Addis and Arnold, The *Catholic Dictionary* (6th ed., Nesyork) 1886.

Enhanced Strong's Lexicon, (Oak Harbor, WA: Logos Research Systems, Inc.) 1995.

Farraris, *Bibliotheca canonica, III* (Rome, Italy) 1886.

Fort Worth StarTelegram, Sunday, January 10, 1999.

Hagan, Kenneth E., *A Midas Touch, A Balanced Approach to Biblical Prosperity,* (Faith Library Publications, Tulsa, OK) 2000.

Henry, Matthew, *Matthew Henry's Commentary on the Bible,* (Peabody, MA: Henderson Publishers) 1991.

Selden, *History of Tithes* (London, England) 1618.

Spelmen, *Of Tyhes* (London, England) 1723.

The King James Version, (Cambridge: Cambridge) 1769.

The New Bible Dictionary, (Wheaton, Illinois: Tyndale House Publishers, Inc.) 1962.

The New International Version, (Grand Rapids, MI: Sondervan Publishing House) 1984.

Walvoord, John F., and Zuck, Roy B., *The Bible Knowledge Commentary,* (Wheaton, Illinois: Scripture Press Publications, Inc.) 1983, 1985.

Webb, Michael L., *Beyond Tithes & Offerings,* (Tacoma, WA: On time Publishing) 1997.

Smith, Jerome, *The New Treasury of the Scripture Knowledge*

Johnson, R., *Lie of the Tithe* (Flagstaff, AZ: Simple Truth Inc., 1999)

Bibliography Internet

Amirault, Gary, *Internet*
Cheong Dr., Eddie, *Internet*
Combs, Dave, *Internet*
Halff Dr., Charles, *Internet*
Krause, Hubert and Soylma, Orest, *History of Tithing from the Bible, Internet*
Morton, Timothy S, *Internet*
Neckar, Andy, *Internet*
Van Druff, Dean, *Internet*
Whitehead, Kevin, *Internet*